ASHEVILLE-BUNCOMBE TECHNICAL INSTITUTE

NORTH CAROLINA
STATE BOARD OF EDUCATION

LLEGES

Discarded
Date MAR 2 5 2024

The
Community
Dimension
of
the
Community
College

The Community Dimension of the Community College

Ervin L. Harlacher

President
Brookdale Community College

PRENTICE-HALL, INC.
Englewood Cliffs, New Jersey

Library of Congress Catalog Card Number 70-82705

Printed in the United States of America
CURRENT PRINTING (LAST DIGIT):
10 9 8 7 6 5 4 3 2

PRENTICE-HALL INTERNATIONAL, INC., *London*
PRENTICE-HALL OF AUSTRALIA, PTY. LTD., *Sydney*
PRENTICE-HALL OF CANADA, LTD., *Toronto*
PRENTICE-HALL OF INDIA PRIVATE LTD., *New Delhi*
PRENTICE-HALL OF JAPAN, INC., *Tokyo*

Preface

Community services is now widely recognized as a major function of the community college. While the community college continues to serve its community through its regular programs and activities, an increasing number of colleges now provide, in cooperation with other community agencies, special programs of community services, i.e., educational, cultural, and recreational services above and beyond regularly scheduled day and evening classes. By so doing, these institutions recognize that by definition the community college has an obligation to:

1. Become a center of community life by encouraging the use of college facilities and services by community groups when such use does not interfere with the college's regularly scheduled programs;
2. Provide for all age groups educational services that utilize the special skills and knowledge of the college staff and other experts and be designed to meet the needs of community groups and the college district community at large;
3. Provide the community, including business and industry, with the leadership and coordination capabilites of the college, assist the community in long-range planning, and join with individuals and groups in attacking unsolved problems;
4. Contribute to and promote the cultural, intellectual, and social life of the college district community and the development of skills for the profitable use of leisure time.

The full potential of the program is not yet realized by all institutions. But there is reason to believe that the next great thrust of community college development will be in the direction of community services. The American Association of Junior Colleges (AAJC), therefore, authorized the present study with four purposes in mind:

1. To identify and report the nature and scope of community services programs currently being provided by U. S. community colleges;
2. To identify and describe exemplary community services programs and/or activities in community colleges in the United States;
3. To identify and report problems, issues, and trends in community college programs of community services;
4. To identify and recommend the appropriate role of the AAJC in the development and/or expansion of community college programs of community services.

With the financial assistance of the Alfred P. Sloan Foundation, I visited, during the summer and fall of 1967, thirty-seven community college districts in thirteen states, representing the small and the large, the rich and the poor, the urban and the rural community college. I also corresponded with administrators of twenty-eight additional college districts in twelve states, with trustees and presidents of newly organized community college districts, and with officials of state agencies concerned with the governance of community colleges. (The sixty-five community college districts participating in this study operate 104 college campuses in nineteen states.)

In conducting this study and preparing the publication, I also drew on the findings of my 1965 nationwide study of programs of community services in ninety-nine colleges in thirty-one states, also sponsored by the AAJC.[1]

In a recent study of public demands made upon boards of trustees of community college districts, the author concluded that:

... the planning and the management of community services is a responsibility that will become increasingly important and this aspect of junior college service should be given as much thought and consideration as some of the more formal academic programs.[2]

Accordingly, it is thought that this study will (1) be of value to new community colleges desirous of inaugurating a program of community services and to existing community colleges wishing to establish or strengthen such programs; (2) contribute toward closing the gap between what is and what ought to be in community college programs of community services; and (3) provide the basis upon which a major position statement of the AAJC regarding the community services function of the community college may be made.

I wish to express my appreciation to administrators and staff members

[1]Ervin Le Roy Harlacher, "Critical Requirements for the Establishment of Effective Junior College Programs of Community Services" (unpublished Ed.D. dissertation, University of California, Los Angeles, 1965).

[2]Walter B. Pentz, "The Effect of Population Changes Upon the Demands Made by the Public of Junior College Trustees" (unpublished Ed.D. dissertation, University of California, Los Angeles, 1967).

in participating community colleges, without whose contributions this study would not have been possible; to officials of the American Association of Junior Colleges for their guidance and general assistance; and to members of the special advisory committee with whom I consulted during the development and editing of this study.

Brookdale Community College   Ervin L. Harlacher
Lincroft, New Jersey
                                               President

Contents

4

What's Past Is Prologue   69

Appendixes   *109*

Members of Advisory Committee

Donald A. Eldridge
President
Bennett College
Millbrook, New York

Sam E. Hand
Director
Continuing Education
Florida State University
Tallahassee, Florida

Cyril O. Houle
Professor of Education
University of Chicago
Chicago, Illinois

B. Lamar Johnson
Professor of Higher Education
University of California
Los Angeles, California

Eugene I. Johnson
Executive Director
Adult Education Association
of U.S.A.
Washington, D. C.

Robert E. Kinsinger
Director
Division of Education
and Public Affairs
W. K. Kellogg Foundation
Battle Creek, Michigan

S. V. Martorana
Executive Dean for Two-Year
Colleges
State University of New York
Albany, New York

Jules Pagano
Director
Division of Adult Education Programs
U. S. Office of Education
Washington, D. C.

Bill J. Priest
Chancellor
Dallas County Junior College District
Dallas, Texas

Maurice F. Seay
Professor of Education
Western Michigan University
Kalamazoo, Michigan

Paul Sheats
Dean-University Extension
University of California
Los Angeles, California

Norman E. Watson
District Superintendent
Orange Coast Junior College District
Costa Mesa, California

The
Community
Dimension
of
the
Community
College

A
Second
Dimension

1

"For God's sake," passionately wrote Sir Walter Moberly nearly twenty years ago, "stop researching for a while and begin to think. We need . . . not only discoverers of facts . . . but explorers of ideas and rethinkers of values . . . we should speak more of the improvement . . . rather than the extension of knowledge. . . . We want more thinking about the importance of things already known" (13:183–84).*

Moberly, the former chairman of the University Grants Committee in England, was addressing himself to university professors, apparently ignoring the fact that a segment of the American public education system was already dedicated to the application of knowledge; that even then the American junior college was, in fact, thinking about the importance of things already known. For, from its very beginnings, this distinctively American institution had assumed the responsibility for providing all persons desiring it with the necessary knowledge to live a fuller, more productive life in a democratic society. It had no intention of repeating the history of the universities; it was determined to trace out boldly its own way with reference to the wants of an emergent society so that it might constantly suffuse that society with fresh thought—thought relative not to nebulous theorizing but to life as it is lived here and now. Recognizing that its services could best be utilized only if it became integrated into the community, the junior college accepted its responsibility to be aware of what was going on in this world of business and industry, as well as in the realm of speculative thought and abstract research. With Plato, it realized that "States are made, not from rocks and trees, but from the character of their citizens. . . ," and it sought to help mold the character of its citizens within its surrounding community.

*Sources appear at the end of each chapter. First number indicates the source; second represents page numbers.

That purpose grew stronger with each passing year; yet its fulfillment remained just beyond reach. To be sure, the junior college classrooms were filled with young people, most of whom were either awaiting admission to colleges empowered to confer the baccalaureate degree or were there to acquire the technical skills necessary for gainful employment. Evening classes served adults bent on self-improvement. Until the last two and a half decades, however, the ideal of reaching the entire community fell short of realization. But even today not all junior colleges are community colleges. Writers frequently contrast the program of a "junior college" to a program of a "community college," recognizing that the two terms are not synonymous.

The junior colleges were first established with the single purpose of offering two years of work acceptable to universities. In fact, at the second meeting of the American Association of Junior Colleges in 1922, junior college was defined as "an institution offering two years of instruction of strictly collegiate grade." Even the term *junior college* implies the function to be served.

Junior college, then, describes an institution that primarily duplicates organizationally and fulfills philosophically the first two years of the four-year senior college. The true community college, on the other hand, connotes an institution that has changed from an isolated entity to one seeking full partnership with its community. In the process, it has become for its district community a cultural center, a focal point of intellectual life, a source of solidarity, a fount of local pride.

In 1955, B. Lamar Johnson, Professor of Higher Education, University of California, Los Angeles, wrote in the Silver Anniversary issue of the *Junior College Journal*: "It is the considered judgment of this author that the most important junior college development of the past twenty-five years has been *the emergence of the concept of the public junior college as a community college*" (9:482–85). Twelve years later he was able to reaffirm that judgment: "In the intervening years, there has been no reason for me to change this view. As a matter of fact, the history of the junior college in recent years has served to accentuate the role of the two-year college as a community institution" (10:5).

James Thornton has characterized the evolution of the community college in three stages, which are related to the major purposes or functions of the institution. The first two stages he refers to as "education for transfer" (1850–1920) and expansion of "occupational programs" (1920–45). The addition of occupational curricula gave the junior college a new complexion. Nonetheless, it did not achieve its full stature as a community college until the development of the third stage, beginning in approximately 1945, when the community services concept apparently saltated into being (17:46–53).

A MULTIPURPOSED INSTITUTION

Although many lists of the purposes of the community college may be found, the vast majority of such colleges, to meet the needs of a changing society, have committed themselves to five major purposes: preparation for advanced study (transfer), occupational education (terminal), general education, guidance and counseling, and community services.

John W. Gardner, former Secretary of Health, Education, and Welfare, had the diversity and flexibility of the community college philosophy and functions in mind when he wrote in 1958:

> The traditionalists might say, of course, let Princeton create a junior college and one would have an institution of unquestionable excellence! That is correct, but it leads us down precisely the wrong path. If Princeton Junior College were excellent in the sense that Princeton University is excellent, it would not be excellent in the most important way that a junior college can and may be excellent. It would simply be a truncated version of Princeton. A comparable meaningless result would be achieved if General Motors tried to add to its line of low-priced cars by marketing the front end of a Cadillac (3:524).

The program of the community college may be thought of as twofold: formal education and informal education. Through its formal dimension, sometimes characterized as schooling, the community college provides transfer, occupational, general education, and guidance and counseling programs for youth and adults enrolled in regularly scheduled day and evening classes on the campus. But it is through its informal, community dimension that the junior college truly becomes a community college. The chief phenomenon accompanying this metamorphosis has been the development of programs of community services.

Chancellor Samuel B. Gould of the State University of New York has underscored the importance of this aspect:

> It is my conviction that a college, in addition to its more readily accepted intellectual dimension, should have the dimension of community that offers a place for the general life enrichment of all who live nearby: young and old, artisan and farmer and member of a profession, college graduate and comparatively unskilled. Thus many of the gaps or weaknesses that the new pressures of numbers are bound to create in formal education can be filled or strengthened as a college opens its doors and its resources to all in a friendly and informal fashion, without thought of credits or degrees or anything more than to assist the burgeoning of understanding in the individual as a member of a personal, physical, political, economic, artistic and spiritual world (4:55–56).

The philosophy that the community college campus encompasses the length and breadth of the college district, and that the total population of the district is its student body, makes it possible for the community college, in a massive and untraditional way, to broaden the base for higher education, to ease the problems of access to higher education by taking the college to the people, and to free itself from the traditional image of the American college and university which sees college primarily, if not entirely, as an institution concerned with educating youth.

In some way the idea became fixed in the American mind that a formal college education supplied sufficient education for a lifetime. Today, in a time of vast knowledge explosion, with men seeking emotional and imaginative fulfillment, this supposition circumvents truth. Education is a continuous and total process of developing the individual to his fullest potential, which is achieved through both formal and informal experiences and interactions.

Looking beyond its formalized classroom and campus(es) to the community college can mean some education for almost everyone, not only for youngsters just out of high school, but also for the body of citizens who received their terminal education some years ago, perhaps from a four-year college, and who are not interested in further degrees or credits; the community college is responsive to changing needs of all segments of its population; it can be for almost everyone the means to raise not just his standard of living but rather his "standard of life." Since the community college aims at the whole person in a whole community, it sees no one as being unworthy because of his present level of development, his ideas, or his current status within the culture.

GENESIS OF
COMMUNITY SERVICE FUNCTION

The community service idea dates from ancient Greece—possibly earlier. Socrates first exemplified it by taking his wisdom into the streets and the marketplace, where he created a student community representative of the people and actively concerned with the social and moral issues of the time. Painting the familiar scene with words as skillful as an artist's brush, Will Durant permits us to see once more

... this ungainly figure, clad always in the same tunic, walking leisurely through the agora, undisturbed by the bedlam of politics, buttonholing his prey, gathering the young and learned about him, luring them into some shady nook of the temple porticos, and asking them to define their terms (2:5).

Though Socrates himself wrote nothing, his concept of community services is reflected in his young friend Plato's *Republic*, which sought to establish an ideal community in which all the people would receive proper education for their respective positions (1:115–83). It was carried forward by Aristotle, teaching Athenian youth in the shaded walks of the Lyceum. The same concept is clearly evident in the teachings of Jesus and His disciples as they wandered from place to place sharing with the multitudes a new philosophy. And it can be seen at work in the universities of the Middle Ages to which young men came from all walks of life.

There was the scion of the princely or noble house [Hastings Rashdall tells us] who lived in the style to which he was accustomed at home ... there was the poor scholar, reduced to beg for his living or to become the servitor of a College or of a Master or well-to-do student. ... But the vast majority of scholars were of a social position intermediate between the highest and the very lowest—sons of knights and yeomen, merchants, butchers, tradesmen or thrifty artisans, nephews of successful ecclesiastics, or promising lads who had attracted the attention of a neighboring Abbott or Archdeacon (14:655–56).

Such were the "clerks" of the Middle Ages, whose purpose it was to administer community services to the commonalty through the dissemination of their own learning to any who would listen.

Such informal instruction as the clerks were able to provide led to the establishment of centers of learning to which persons thirsting for knowledge traveled from far and near. Although instruction remained without benefit of organized course work, the universities did advance the principle of education for all who would join their student communities. Thus, with the founding of the university at Bologna late in the eleventh century, higher education in Western Europe came to life. Through cycles of support, conflict, hostility, and somnolence, the universities remained intimately tied up with the life of the society of which they had become a part.

By the eighteenth century, the idea of providing higher education for all the people had been abandoned, and the universities became storehouses for factual knowledge and retreats for the idle rich or select few. Nicholas Hans saw "an appalling wastage of talent in the eighteenth century," when "Classical education . . . , divorced from science, became simply a sign of social privilege. Scientific education, narrowed down to technical skill, lost its broader emancipating appeal and was avoided by cultured families" (6:210–12). The deterioration of the universities witnessed during this period evoked David Hume's fervent hope that "the present evil phenomena [observed in the English universities] are rectified in other regions," and prompted J. J. Rousseau to speak with contempt of institutions of higher learning in France (18:386). In essence the universities of eighteenth-century Western Europe had sunk into what Robert Hutchins has called "a deep torpor from which they would not awaken for more than a hundred and fifty years" (8:97), a sentiment echoed by another historian: "It was not difficult to prove that, in 1820, the old universities were not satisfying, and could not satisfy, the increasing needs of the new age" (15:19).

Nor could the "old universities" in America, patterned as they were after the European institutions, satisfy the requirements of the "new age" in the New World. Here, in vast expanses of wilderness where communities were loosely knit in terms of boundaries and where the people were engaged in the all-absorbing business of creating a nation, lay fertile fields for the development of community services.

The first step toward providing such services was taken in 1826 by Josiah Holbrook of Derby, Connecticut, when he established the American Lyceum, dedicated to the principle of citizen participation in community development, the importance of a community climate of problem-solving on a face-to-face basis, and the utilization of educational resources to solve practical problems. Named after the Athenian garden near the temple of Apollo Lyceus where Aristotle had lectured to the youth of Greece, the Lyceum answered a widely felt need. Within the first eight years of its existence, 3,000 branches were established in nearly every state of the Union. In later years, after the Lyceum died out, the Chautauqua, initiated in 1874, carried forward the Lyceum "spirit" and became a symbol of education and culture until its peak year in 1924 (11:329–32). By that time, the American junior college had already entered its second stage of development.

There seems little doubt that two other movements, the community school concept in the public schools and the community development concept in the four-year institutions of higher learning, have had a profound influence on the development of the community college and its community service function.

Two distinct emphases characterized what was initially known as the community school concept: (1) service to the whole community, not merely to the children attending the schools, and (2) "discovery, development, and use of the resources of the community as part of the educational facilities of the school" (16:209). This concept of service to the total community is significant, for the easy course is to limit the school's program to the students and perhaps the parents. However, authorities estimate that from 40 to 60 percent of the community's voting citizens are not parents of public school children. Thus, it seemed obvious that, if the schools were to fulfill their assigned function of community improvement, they had to be closely attuned to the lives of the people they served— including the 40 to 60 percent. But, despite this apparent awareness of their prescribed role, not all schools have become "community schools." Many of them stand apart from the major current of cultural growth, thus limiting their influence and courting isolation.

At the other end of the educational spectrum, community development in four-year institutions of higher education, usually administered as a part of university extension, was conceived to be "a process of community education and action democratically organized and carried through by the people themselves to reach goals they hold in common for the improvement of the entire community" (12:14). The concept of helping people to help themselves was not new. The American Lyceum and the Chautauqua had already demonstrated its effectiveness. But another step in its development was taken with the establishment of agricultural extension as a function of American universities under the Morrill Act (1862) and the Smith-Lever Acts (1914). During the 1940's, a number of pilot projects in four-year institutions of higher education helped to define and popularize community development as a specialized function of higher education. Nevertheless, the universities tended to remain selective so that programs of community development reached only certain segments of the population.

COMMUNITY SERVICE AGENCY

The community college is an American social institution growing out of the nation's unique social, political, economic, and cultural society and its needs. Its growth is one of the most revolutionary, exciting, and vital developments in the history of American education. Although, in the chain of institutions established to perform the function of education, our society has created the university on one end and the school on the other, the community college is neither a school nor a university. It has developed as the result of the apparent inability of the high school and the university to adapt rapidly enough to changing needs, thus acquiring an identity of its own and a unique role to play in education. The community college is also characterized by two distinct qualities when compared to other institutions in the United States: (1) it is of comparatively recent origin with its greatest growth occurring since 1920; (2) its birth and development are indigenous to this country.

The original idea of the community college was one that involved a grass roots approach. In theory, at least, everyone connected with such an institution would look around, find educational gaps, and help fill the gaps. The community college faculty and staff—teachers and doers in the broadest possible sense—undertake to solve human problems in the community around them or point out the needs to other local educational groups.

Rooted in the soil of the district community it serves and drawing its students and strength from that community, the community college is particularly suited as a community service agency. Baker Brownell, emeritus professor of philosophy at Northwestern University, has said of the community college:

It should be a resource not only for classroom studies, but for the many services, cultural, occupational, and professional, which are possible in such a situation but are not yet realized by many colleges (7:318).

Several characteristics of the community college uniquely qualify it to offer these services:

(1) The community college is a community-centered institution with the primary purpose of providing service to the people of its community. Its offerings and programs are planned to meet the needs of the community and are developed with the active participation of citizens.

Colleges and universities have traditionally served large geographic areas (e.g., an entire state). In consequence, it has been difficult if not impossible for them to establish a sense of "community" even with people living relatively nearby. The result has been indifference and a strengthening of the concept that they are exclusively compounds for educating young people.

The school, church, family, business, labor, etc., have tended to go separate ways, developing almost in isolation from each other; American life has become fragmented as well as specialized. There has been no force to draw the basic institutions together, to give to each other the uniqueness that each possesses. So geographic communities have existed without "community"—without a real concern and commitment within each institution for each other institution, without a sense of community among heterogeneous people.

(2) The community college claims and develops community service to be one of its major functions.

(3) Since the community college is usually a creature of citizens of the local community or area, and since it is most frequently governed by a board of local citizens, the community college is readily capable of responding to changing community needs.

(4) Most community colleges are operated by a local district that encompasses several separate and distinct communities. The ideal locale for a program of community services is one "in which there are numerous communities and sub-communities with natural and compelling interrelationships . . ." (16:144). The program of community services welds these separate communities and groups together without submerging individual identities.

(5) The community college is an institution of higher education and, as such, can draw upon the advanced resources of its staff to assist in the solution of the problems of an increasingly complex society.

(6) The community college, as a relatively new segment of American

education, is unencrusted with tradition, unfettered by a rigid history, eager for adventure. Therefore, without duplicating existing services in the community, it is able to tailor its program to meet local needs and conditions.

The community college, then—if it will only emphasize its uniqueness, freedom from tradition, and dynamic qualities—has a chance to do what the four-year colleges have not done because it works as one of a number of cooperating agencies to meet community needs without usurping the roles or functions of others. It is disinterested in terms of the community power structure, it has no profit motive, it has no axe to grind, and it has the human resources to do the job. It is the unified force that casts aside red tape, apathy, jealousies, and asks what the community problems are and how "all of us together solve them."

The true community college is not just concerned with the schooling of college-age youth and adults enrolled in transfer and occupational programs: it accepts the responsibility as a catalytic agent for stimulating efforts toward enrichment and development of the college district community as a whole, through the mobilization of elements of the total community. And the community college further accepts responsibility for the educational growth of all individuals in its community, regardless of whether or not they are enrolled in formalized classes.

SELECTED REFERENCES

1. Commins, Saxe, and Robert N. Linscott, eds., *The Social Philosophers.* New York: Barron's Series, Inc., 1948.

2. Durant, Will, *The Story of Philosophy.* New York: Simon and Schuster, 1926.

3. Gardner, John W., "Quality in Higher Education," *Junior College Journal* XXVII (May 1958).

4. Gould, Samuel B., *Knowledge is Not Enough.* Yellow Springs, Ohio: Antioch Press, 1959.

5. Hamlin, Herbert M., *Citizens' Committees in the Public Schools.* Danville, Ill.: The Interstate Printers and Publishers, 1952.

6. Hans, Nicholas, *New Trends in Education in the Eighteenth Century.* London: Routledge and Kegan Paul, 1951.

7. Henry, Nelson B., ed., *The Public Junior College.* 55th Yearbook, National Society for the Study of Education. Chicago: The University of Chicago Press, 1956.

8. Hutchins, Robert M., *The Conflict in Education.* New York: Harper & Brothers, 1953.

9. Johnson, B. Lamar, "An Emerging Concept Points to the Future," *Junior College Journal* XXV (April 1955).

10. Johnson, B. Lamar, "Preface" in Ervin L. Harlacher, *Effective Junior College Programs of Community Services: Rationale, Guidelines, Practices,* Junior College Leadership Program, Occasional Report Number 10. Los Angeles: School of Education, University of California, 1967.

11. Jones, Bertis L., *The History of Community Development in American Universities With Particular Reference to Four Selected Institutions.* Unpublished Ed.D. dissertation, University of California, Los Angeles, 1961.

12. Lackey, Katherine, *Community Development Through University Extension.* Carbondale, Ill.: Southern Illinois University, 1960.

13. Moberly, Sir Walter, *The Crisis in the University.* London: S.C.M. Press, 1949.

14. Rashdall, Hastings, *The Universities of Europe in the Middle Ages.* Oxford: The Clarendon Press, 1895.

15. Robertson, C. G., *The British Universities.* London: Methuen, 1944.

16. Seay, Maurice F., and Ferris N. Crawford, *The Community School and Community Self-Improvement.* Lansing, Mich.: Clair L. Taylor, Superintendent of Public Instruction, 1954.

17. Thornton, James W., Jr., *The Community Junior College.* New York: John Wiley and Sons, 1960.

18. Ulich, Robert, *Three Thousand Years of Educational Wisdom.* Cambridge, Mass.: Harvard University Press, 1954.

Beyond
The
Formal
Curriculum

2

The community college is committed by its philosophy to serve all segments of its community. The attempt to satisfy community needs has led to wide acceptance of community service as a major function of this truly unique institution of higher education.

There is no doubt that the community college provides community services through many of its regular programs and activities, including the development of curricula based on identified community needs. But an increasing number of colleges are coming to realize the necessity for developing programs specifically directed toward providing educational, cultural, and recreational services for their communities over and beyond regularly scheduled day and evening classes. This awareness stems from the fact that community services extend beyond those bound in with the formal education program.

Baker Brownell has suggested the community service role of the community college as

The junior college in its role as a community college should serve students of all ages and occupations within the context of the student's community and occupation.

It should be a resource not only for classroom studies but for the many services, cultural, occupational, and professional, which are possible in such a situation but are not yet realized fully by many colleges (8:818).

DEFINITION OF
COMMUNITY SERVICES

Many different definitions of community services are to be found in the literature of the junior college movement. Although these definitions differ in precise content, they encompass essentially the same concept. James

11

Reynolds, for example, views community services as "involving both college and community resources and conducted for the purpose of meeting specified educational needs of individuals or enterprises within the college or the community" (16:142). Less specifically, but perhaps by implication more inclusively, Leland Medsker (13) and B. Lamar Johnson (10) define community services as "various special services" which the two-year college may provide for its community outside formalized classroom instruction. And Roosevelt Basler considers them to be "the provision of a variety of services to the community through media other than courses and regular classes" (1:428). The definition of community services used in my book is essentially an amalgam of the foregoing; namely, community services are educational, cultural, and recreational services which an educational institution may provide for its community in addition to its regularly scheduled day and evening classes.

Confusion over the definition of community services stems from at least two misconceptions: (1) that community services and adult or continuing education are synonymous, and (2) that the community services program constitutes a program of educational public relations. In actuality, these views are grounded in half-truths and seem to imply that the objectives of community services, adult or continuing education, and public relations have become entangled. Although all three programs are interrelated, each more properly should be considered on its own merits, which suggests the need for careful differentiation and definition of these terms.

In its broadest meaning, adult education as advocated by Paul Sheats, Clarence Jayne, and Ralph Spence would encompass many of the activities included in a program of community services: "the kind of . . . education that will increase and improve citizen participation in decision-making, that will lead to the enrichment of community living, that will release the full power of a society rooted in respect for human dignity and the sanctity of human personality" (17:v). Perhaps the expression of this concept has led some writers to believe that the community service function actually emerged from adult education. The truth is, however, that the two programs are not synonymous, and in recent years they have increasingly been treated in the literature as two separate functions. This may be accounted for by the fact that most community colleges, recognizing the need for adult education in their communities, provide evening programs for those who, for various reasons, cannot become regular full-time day students. But these programs are often little more than formalized evening classes for adults.

One of the reasons community services are identified with adult education is that the program, particularly in the smaller community colleges, has often been administered by the administrator of the adult or evening college program. Unfortunately, it frequently happened that this person, immersed in the details of the formal adult education program, did not have the time to develop an additional program. As a result, the community services responsibility of the college was assumed to have been fulfilled if, in a passive way, evening courses were opened to adults, or if a new course—any kind of course—was offered "any time ten or more citizens want it, if teacher, space, funds, and equipment are available" (19:47).

That the dual administration of community services and evening college programs in American community colleges is largely a phenomenon of the past was evident in my study. Of the thirty-seven community college districts I visited, all but eleven (70%) provided for separate administration of the two programs.

Adult education, as properly defined, may be classified as one type of community service. However, it should be considered as only one of many services and it requires something more than just offering fancy cooking courses.

The recent substitution of the synonym *continuing education* for *adult education* has also added to the confusion surrounding these terms. In community colleges across the country, continuing education is variously defined as those noncredit short courses offered by the community services division, all noncredit adult education offerings, college credit courses offered in the evening for adults, both credit and noncredit offerings for adults, curricular-based noncredit courses for adults, special courses day and evening for students enrolled in less than college-level work, and courses offered at the community college for currently enrolled high school students.

As a matter of fact, *continuing education* would be an appropriate term to describe the entire formal education program of the community college, for adults are found in all phases of the program, day and evening. Some take preparatory courses for transferral to senior colleges or universities; others take occupational courses to improve themselves in their work or obtain the associate degree; and many take courses to broaden their educational and cultural experiences or utilize leisure time more effectively.

Programs of community services differ from adult education in still another way. They are not limited to adults of the community, but are provided for persons of all ages, occupations, and levels of educational development, including high school students, elementary students, and even preschool children in some cases.

The point of view that the program of community services is merely a public relations vehicle for communicating with the institution's external public is also not only mistaken but fraught with danger. A truly effective community services program is unlimited in either function or scope, while public relations—at least as normally characterized—is more concerned with the perpetuation of the organization than with providing educational services for the community. There is, of course, one important relationship between community services and the college's over-all public relations. Unquestionably, a comprehensive program of community services, developed in response to community needs and with community participation, will have a profound effect upon the college's public image. Jesse Bogue has made this point clearly:

Even if the college is thinking only in terms of enlightened self-interest, its services to adults can be, as they have proved to be in many communities, one of the surest and soundest ways to build strong and favorable public relations. Many of the problems now facing public school systems owing to the indifference of taxpayers could be resolved by services to the adults of the community (2:229).

In fact, wherever the community services program has been highly developed, the college has been able to consolidate the interests of town and gown to the extent that it has met with few difficulties in securing community support for meeting its needs (18:246). Moreover, because the college's influence within its community is closely related to its prestige there, the effectiveness of its public relations will be in direct proportion to the effectiveness and comprehensiveness of its community services program. To an important degree, this program determines the level of community support for the total college program.

The community services function as defined in this study is completely foreign to the traditional idea of college education; it is the manifestation for which the community college was created. Moreover, in most community colleges, the number of persons served by the program of community services exceeds vastly the number served through the regular transfer and occupational programs offered for youth and adults. As an example, a California community college reported that total attendance in the program of community services for the year was in excess of 200,000, while day and evening enrollment in the college totaled 12,000.

The nature and scope of the program of community services was spelled out in the 55th Yearbook of the National Society for the Study of Education, *The Public Junior College*:

The values of college service to the community ... include increasing the productive efficiency of agriculture and industry, improving the functioning of communities and community organizations, contributing to the health and physical well-being of citizens, and enriching the cultural, aesthetic, and moral life of the community (8:72).

And Reynolds has listed two characteristics of community service activities: (1) each activity is provided to help satisfy a genuine educational need in the community; (2) the chief beneficiaries of each of the activities are citizens of the community (16:143).

IMPLEMENTATION
OF COMMUNITY SERVICES

Implementation of the community services function entails acceptance of the following principles: (1) In a community college the campus is the length and breadth of the junior college district. (2) The program of community services is designed to bring the community to the college and take the college program out into the community. (3) The educational program of the college must not be limited to formalized classroom instruction. (4) The community college recognizes its responsibility as a catalyst in community development and self-improvement. (5) The program of community services meets community needs and does not duplicate existing services in the community (6:15).

Through its program of community services, the community college can bind together the separate and diverse communities that make up a community college district or service area, producing a close interrelationship of college and community. But for the program to achieve its maximum potential, the close cooperation of citizens and community agencies—educational, cultural, recreational, professional, industrial—is required. Thus, the community college in providing a special program of community services assumes, not the relatively passive role of offering classes for adults, but that of a catalytic force, supplying the leadership, coordination, and cooperation necessary to stimulate action programs by appropriate individuals and groups within the community.

In its most significant role, the program of community services constitutes what might be called *Operation Outreach*. Since community services extend far beyond mere post-high school education and are designed to serve all age groups, both on the campus and out in the community, the outreach aspect of such programs appears to be self-evident. If the community college is fully to achieve its purposes, then, it must move out into the community to create a program. Adult or continuing education programs, as traditionally administered by community colleges, are not designed to meet this need; they are preoccupied with offering standard credit courses to meet educational needs unrelieved in previous high school or college programs.

The comprehensive nature of programs of community services is illustrated in the following description of a mythical California community college, synthesized from actual practices observed in several colleges by

Hugh G. Price, former chief of the Bureau of Junior College Education, California State Department of Education:

Since its organization in 1935, El Dorado Junior College has become a cultural center for Golddust County. Fine musical and dramatic performances by college student groups and a variety of programs by individuals and groups with state-wide and national reputations have been presented in its 1500 seat auditorium. Performances by symphony orchestras, vocal and instrumental soloists, dancers, dramatic groups, and choral groups; various forums and lectures on cultural, literary, travel and political topics—all these have drawn audiences. . . . Leadership by members of the college administration and faculty in churches, service clubs, community councils and committees has been of great value to these agencies. The community relies upon the college to cooperate with it in solving major problems that arise. Both the college faculty and students participate in community activities, such as campaigning and raising funds for the community chest; dealing with problems of juvenile delinquency, and zoning, organizing, and operating youth centers; getting out the vote at elections; protecting the water supply; and helping to plan for the beautification of streets and parks and for adequate police and fire protection (15:15–16).

EXPANSION OF
COMMUNITY SERVICES PROGRAMS

Throughout the nation, increasing recognition of community service as a major function of the community college has brought with it widespread expansion of programs of community services. As early as 1960, Medsker reported that 219 (90%) of the 243 U.S. community colleges included in his 1956 study indicated that they were performing a wide variety of "the unusual services that make an institution a community college" (13:79). These he listed under eleven major categories:

1. Widespread use of the college physical plant by community groups.
2. Assistance by college in safety and thrift campaigns, fund drives, and the like.
3. Organization of special events, such as workshops, institutes, forums, for business, professional, or governmental groups for the purpose of either in-service training of employees or the general improvement of the group.
4. Promotion of cultural and recreational activities, such as the development of community musical groups, sponsoring of little theater groups.
5. Promotion by the college of community events in which public affairs are discussed.
6. Organization projects with other community agencies relating to the improvement of health conditions in the community.

7. Use of the college staff and students in making studies of the community (such as occupational surveys, sociological studies).

8. Widespread use of college staff as speakers to community groups.

9. Organization of services using staff or students, or films and lectures from outside, to further the conservation of natural resources.

10. Research by college staff and students for business or professional groups in the community.

11. Organization of child-care programs for demonstration and instructional purposes.

On the basis of his visits to the colleges, however, Medsker was forced to the conclusion that in many instances these services were not performed frequently.

Nevertheless, institutional concern for meeting the needs of the entire community was making itself increasingly manifest. Perhaps nowhere in the nation was that concern more evident than in California, whose community colleges long have led the nation in the development of comprehensive programs of community services. In examining the catalogs of sixty-nine California public junior colleges in the fall of 1964, for example, it was discovered that forty (58%) of them claimed community service as a major function, and that ten included it under a related function—most frequently adult education (5:50). And a later study in the same year of the state's seventy-one public junior colleges showed that 70 percent provided community use of facilities, cultural programs, campus conferences, public affairs lectures, speakers' bureaus, short courses, community recreation, campus tours, and special events (6).

Few California community colleges do not offer community services as a major function, as indicated in a 1966–67 survey report prepared by the California Junior College Association's Committee on Community Services (3). Of the state's sixty-six college districts fifty-one (77%) responded. These districts operate sixty campuses. Information was elicited concerning types and frequency of community service offerings as well as the administrative personnel.

Of the sixty campuses, forty-one had at least one person assigned full time to the administration of community services, and twelve anticipated the addition of a full-time administrator the following year. In the fifty-one districts, forty-six levied part or all of the 5-cent community services tax. This tax was utilized to support the community services program as follows (median %): civic center (use of facilities) expenditures, 18.5 percent, community educational services, 8.5 percent; recreation, 7 percent; and "other" (primarily capital outlay), 20.8 percent.

Community services were reported by the sixty campuses in the following categories, listed in rank order: community performance events; faculty-student programs; recreation; noncredit short courses, seminars, workshops, conferences, institutes; art festivals; community research and development; community counseling and consultative services; planetarium and museum shows; and radio-television.

On sixteen campuses it was estimated that fifty to ninety-nine community organizations used the campus facilities during the year; nine campuses gave an estimate of 100 to 299; and replies on four questionnaires indicated 300 to 699 organizations had been so accommodated. Utilization to the extent reported was, of course, not the general rule. Nevertheless, some 3,526,000 Californians participated in community services programs on the sixty campuses during 1966–67 as follows: community use of facilities, 1,808,000; recreation, 808,000; community forums and lecture series, 269,000; fine arts series, 224,000; community performance events, 199,000; planetarium and museum shows, 78,000; noncredit short courses, seminars, workshops, conferences, and institutes, 72,000; arts festivals, 50,000; and community research and development projects, 18,000.

Over-all expansion of the community services function was expected to command the strongest effort for the ensuing year on twenty-two campuses and twenty-five were going to concentrate on developing a specific aspect of the program. On all campuses the total effort seemed to be toward expansion and the development of new programs to match currently successful ones (3).

This effort was consistent with the general expansion of the community services function confirmed in a nationwide survey conducted by this author in 1965. Of 126 community colleges in the United States that claimed community services as a major function, responses were received from ninety-nine (88 public, 11 private) colleges. Population areas varied from 2,500 to 1,000,000 or more. Full-time enrollments in the colleges ranged from under 500 to over 10,000.

Twenty-eight categories of community services were reported by these community colleges in four major areas: community use of college facilities, community educational services, cultural and recreational activities, and institutional development. Nearly all of the responding colleges (96%) claimed inclusion of all four objective areas in their programs of community services. Of the public community colleges included, eighty-six listed Community Educational Services and Institutional Development as program objectives, eighty-five named Cultural and Recreational Activities, and seventy-nine claimed Community Use of College Facilities. Among the private community colleges, all four objective areas were claimed by all except one college, which omitted only Institutional Development in its program.

Most frequently reported (70% or more) community service categories in all four major objective areas are, in rank order: provision of facilities for meetings and conference; cultural programs; educational workshops, seminars, conferences; news service; provision of facilities for community-sponsored cultural events; citizens' advisory committees; and utilization of physical and human resources of the community in the instructional program (7).

OBJECTIVES OF THE
PROGRAM OF COMMUNITY SERVICES

On the basis of a survey of related literature, the results of the nation-wide survey of community services just reported, and the present study, four major objectives of the program of community services provided by U.S. community colleges were identified:

1. To become a center of community life by encouraging the use of college facilities and services by community groups when such use does not interfere with the college's regular schedule;

2. To provide for all age groups educational services that utilize the special skills and knowledge of the college staff and other experts and are designed to meet the needs of community groups and the college district at large;

3. To provide the community, including business and industry, with the leadership and coordination capabilities of the college, assist the community in long-range planning, and join with individuals and groups in attacking unsolved problems;

4. To contribute to and promote the cultural, intellectual, and social life of the college district community and the development of skills for the profitable use of leisure time.

In the following section, each objective of the program of community services is discussed briefly and illustrated with exemplary community services provided by community colleges throughout the country.

I. Community Use of College Facilities and Services

The first objective area of the program of community services includes the categories of physical facilities and services, cosponsorship of community events and activities, community use of library facilities, and campus tours.

As a community center—a gathering place for many community functions—the community college serves one of its most useful purposes. In accordance with state and/or local regulations, college facilities are made available to authorized community groups when they are not used for the college's instructional program. Moreover, the "civic center" policy of community colleges helps to accomplish three important objectives: It provides a part of the solution for an urgent community need. It guarantees that available facilities are used to a fuller percentage of capacity. It serves to acquaint area residents with their community college in the best way possible—through first-hand experience and interaction with the college (14:390).

Planning is essential in developing this service; the community use of college facilities should not be allowed to grow without direction. Through a planned and balanced community center program it is possible to bring to the college campus a wide variety of educational, cultural, and recreational events at no cost to the college. The college-initiated and sponsored community services may then be designed to complement those services already available in the community.

Provision of physical facilities and services: It has been said that the success of the community college can be measured by the extent to which the community makes full use of its facilities. Thus, included in this category is the use of college facilities by scores of community organizations for a wide variety of educational, cultural, recreational, and social activities such as meetings, conferences, concerts, films, lectures, dramatic productions, exhibits, physical activities, and athletic competition. Many colleges also provide food services at minimum cost—luncheons, dinners, receptions, teas—in connection with community-sponsored events held on the campus.

Foothill College in California, for example, makes its facilities available to community groups when they are not being used for its instructional program, in accordance with California's Civic Center Act. With the cooperation of community groups, a balanced and comprehensive cultural program has been planned and the college has become a gathering place for many community functions. During the 1966–67 academic year, sixty-one community groups sponsored 414 events on the Foothill College campus; total attendance at the events during the year was 115,000. Of these community-sponsored events, fifty-six were of a cultural nature and attracted 40,000 persons.

Cultural events range from an annual series of concerts by the San Francisco Symphony to youth symphony concerts, opera, ballet and modern dance, chamber music, drama, vocal recitals, appreciation concerts for children, and art exhibits. These community-sponsored events are in addition to a college-sponsored series of cultural events, art films, and art exhibits, and are in no part financed by the college.

Three community symphony orchestras, the California Youth Symphony, Sunnyvale Orchestra, and Peninsula Symphony Association, use the Foothill campus facilities for both rehearsal and performance. The San

Francisco Symphony uses the 2,700-seat gymnasium for an annual series of nine concerts. Like other organizations that charge admission to their events, the Symphony is required to pay a fee for use of the facilities. No charge is made, however, to those organizations whose events are free to the public.

Extensive community demand for use of facilities necessitated the employment of a full-time supervisor of special services, responsible for scheduling such use, and an auditoriums manager who works with community representatives in making arrangements for the availability of Foothill auditoriums. The college also operates a box office with a full-time manager to handle tickets for both college- and community-sponsored events.

Cosponsorship of community events on campus: One of the most salient services a community college can offer is to join frequently with community groups in the cosponsorship of events and programs staged on the college campus. When this is done, charges for facilities and services are usually waived. Cosponsored events include conferences, special events, educational programs of affiliated organizations, cultural activities, and recreational activities. Although the college may initiate the use of its facilities and services, its participation in a given event or program more frequently is in response to a community request.

Montgomery Junior College, in Maryland, has affiliated with the Metropolitan Washington School of Printing in offering noncredit courses in printing technology for county students. According to the cooperative agreement of March 1966, Montgomery Junior College provides, rent-free, laboratory and classroom space and other facilities at its campus. In return the Metropolitan Washington School of Printing has installed equipment valued at about $100,000 in MJC's technical building for use by all classes.

The program, developed after five years of planning and a survey of technical occupation needs, is geared to the needs of the largest single industry in the area. In September 1966, the MWSP began its tenth year with 175 students housed on the Rockville campus of the college. In 1967–68 it increased enrollment 15 percent and added two new courses. Noncredit courses offered for certificates in either Press or Offset Photography are Introduction to the Graphic Arts, Offset Platemaking, Offset Presswork I and II, Survey of Lithography, Offset Stripping and Negative Work, Offset Photography, Line, and Offset Photography, Halftone.

Community use of library facilities: This community service category covers the use of college library facilities by citizens of the college district community.

Mount San Antonio College in Los Angeles County provides library service for residents of the community college district. Although the library is maintained primarily for enrolled students and personnel of the college, an adult from the community may apply for a pass that enables him to use the library materials within the building. If he is a paid-up member of the Alumni Association, he is entitled to full library privileges.

Area high school students may use the library if they have a referral slip from a high school librarian. Any adult or student from another college may visit the library once with no charge. If he wishes to use the facilities further, however, he must apply for an annual pass and pay a two dollar fee, which entitles him to use the materials in the library building.

To facilitate community use of library service, Mount San Antonio College has employed a full-time community services librarian with funds made available from the restricted community services tax levied by the college district.

Campus tours: Included in this category are organized tours of the college campus in general and special features and programs of the college provided for community groups and individuals.

An example of an outstanding and unusual tour program is provided by State University of New York, Agricultural and Technical Colleges at Farmingdale, in its farm tours. The campus, which is a huge farm, constitutes a living museum on Long Island. Conducted in cooperation with local schools, hourly guided tours are scheduled for bus loads of school youngsters. An estimated 1,000 bus loads of children made the trip to the farm last year, accounting for most of the nearly 32,000 persons who participated in the farm tour program. First through sixth graders in 147 different schools visited the campus under the aegis of the college's Center for Community Educational Services.

Three paid tour guides conduct the lecture-tours of the botanical gardens, farm areas, and animal complex. Included are many brief but exciting lessons that add a new facet to the development of the pupils. Special tours for retarded children have been devised, as well as tours for the blind who explore the campus through their senses of touch and smell.

II. Community Educational Services

The second objective of the program of community services includes noncredit short courses, college credit extension courses, in-service training, community counseling, human resource development training, community consultation, campus radio-television stations, and provisions of faculty and student programs.

College is no longer for youth alone, nor is the educational program of the community college limited to formalized classroom instruction. Community educational services are designed to serve all age groups both on campus and out in the community. These include professionals, and those in search of a profession; executives, and workers aspiring to become executives; the disadvantaged who have been denied higher education because of race or color or because of inability to qualify; housewives and husbands; children and high school age youth.

An objective of the community college is educating for the good of total society. Responding to a swiftly changing social and occupational environment, the true community college gives to its community the learning that man has accumulated: "the arts and sciences that are our greatest weapons in the perpetual war against poverty of the mind and body."

But the community college can no longer be guided by the standard curriculum practices of academically oriented institutions. Educational offerings must be flexible to meet special needs, regardless of hour of day, confines of semester, or granting of so-called college credit. As Samuel B. Gould has pointed out, "The increase of leisure time, the speedily obsolescing elements of training in professional and technical careers, the growing appetite for intellectual development, the effects of automation, the reconsideration of the place of women in our society—these combine to create a new importance for continuing education of many sorts . . ." (4).

Noncredit short courses: Community services short courses include a wide variety of seminars, workshops, symposia, institutes, conferences, and special lectures designed to meet the needs of specific groups and individuals in the college district community. These short courses usually do not offer college credit, and range in length from all-day events to a series covering several weeks. Besides short courses for such diverse groups as parents of handicapped children, parents of young children, club personnel, farmers, women seeking to enter the labor market, senior citizens, and children of the community, the colleges included in this survey developed short courses in specific fields of endeavor.

For business groups the colleges offered short courses in business management, taxation, real estate, restaurant management, export expansion, tourism, banking, purchasing agents, insurance, and executive training. For industry, the short courses developed covered such subjects as fire prevention and plant protection, data processing, housing, basic hydraulics, and plant supervision. Short courses for the professions were paramedical, physician-lawyer relationships, nursing, medical office assistants, community health, "New Concepts in Biology for Elementary Science Teachers," playground theory and practice, securities and investments for teachers, and hospital management. Finally, in the area of government, short courses included area community planning, public utilities, law enforcement, and game wardens.

The College of San Mateo in California has developed perhaps the most imaginative general education oriented short course program in the country. Emphasizing an interdisciplinary approach, the college through its Community Education Program makes a contribution toward raising the "standard of life" of some 10,000 community residents each year.

A major objective of the program is to attack the apparent cultural disintegration associated with increased mobility, affluence, and leisure, through carefully planned lecture series, institutes, seminars, film series, field studies, and other media. Representative titles for short courses include "Youth's Struggle for Identity," "Man and Woman's Search for One Another," "Over-Privileged Youth in an Affluent Society," "Paths to Human Understanding," "Is Man Alone in the Universe?" and "Hinduism and Buddhism: The Impact of Religion on Art." For these short courses and others, such thought leaders as Marshall McLuhan, Pearl Buck, Dr. Max Kaplan, Saul Alinsky, Rollo May, and Sir Alex Douglas-Home were obtained. Plans are also being made to include field studies for a California history short course in the Mother Lode country and the Mission Trail following inauguration of the field studies program in 1967–68 in Death Valley and Mexico City.

Most of the Community Education short courses during the 1966–67 academic year were staged off-campus using schools, churches, the California Teachers Association building, a music auditorium, Department of Public Health and Welfare and the like—often in cooperation with community organizations. In this way the college has become a dynamic partner with groups and institutions within its community.

The College of San Mateo, through its program of Community Education, is providing a model for other community colleges. According to the administrator of the program, "True community as an intangible, creative force for individual and cultural renewal is emerging to take the place of community identity merely as a geographic place." He added that the human work of the community will increasingly be accomplished by local people as the result of awakened community colleges that see their "true mission as nothing less than the evoking of a new tone of mind in a sufficient number of individuals to infect the whole."

Also noteworthy are the program of short courses for farmers offered by Abraham Baldwin Agricultural College, Georgia; and the Institute and Clinic program developed for metropolitan Milwaukee by the Milwaukee Institute of Technology. (See Appendix E for a description of these programs.)

College credit extension courses: The community college campus is not limited to existing campus facilities, but extends throughout the entire college district. Consistent with the philosophy of taking education to the people, a number of community colleges offer college credit courses in off-campus centers.

Representative of these colleges is Miami-Dade Junior College in Florida, which offers college credit courses in a variety of community locations, including airline companies, public agencies, hotels, the Miami Beach Center, and a local Air Force base. The college has offered as many as thirty different college credit classes at the request of local business and government agencies, with more courses being offered during the day than during the evening.

Approximately 600 persons were enrolled in the college credit courses offered through extension during the fall, 1967, by the two campuses of Miami-Dade. Of these students 175 were airmen enrolled in nine different courses at Homestead Air Force Base Center. The program was started as a noncredit program in 1963. Courses are now offered at both freshman and sophomore levels, and the goal is to make it possible for the men to earn an associate degree right at the base.

In the fall of 1967, 125 students were enrolled in four credit courses offered by the college at a local airline company in Miami. Classes were scheduled so that one-half the class period was on company time. This necessitated leaving work one and one-half hours early or reporting one and one-half hours late. The airline paid for half the $10 per credit hour tuition fee upon the worker's successful completion of the course. Half of the 125 students were working towards an associate degree. Forty-five have requested a degree in management. Some 214 persons have taken advantage of the opportunity to earn college credits since the program began in 1965. Average class enrollment is twenty-four. The term coincides with the regular college term. Many persons who would not otherwise do so take college courses available to them at their place of work. Promotion and/or salary review and increase often result from these betterment programs.

In-service training: With the speedily obsolescing elements of training in professional and technical careers and the effects of automation, many community organizations need both consultation and instruction in improving the quality of their personnel. The community college has become the central agency for this service, making competent members of its staff available to companies and agencies for the purpose of upgrading their personnel. In many cases these companies and agencies pay all costs involved for these in-service training programs.

New York City Community College in Brooklyn provides one of the most comprehensive in-service training programs in the country for human service occupations. Examples:

—An eight-week building inspectors training program, begun in July 1966 and funded under Title I of the Higher Education Act of 1965 with an initial grant of $49,000, offered pre-service training for 180 new building inspectors. This training included report writing, conversational

Spanish, social relationships, etc. During the second year the program was extended to include in-service training for 300 existing building inspectors, under a new Title I grant of $55,000. This second-year program also served as a guide for the Building Department in setting up its own training program.

—In cooperation with the district labor council, preparation courses for civil service promotion examinations were conducted for seventy-five candidates. In-service training to upgrade the skills of municipal employees has also been initiated with an anticipated enrollment of 700.

—In response to a serious outbreak of salmonellosis and other types of food poisoning, the college in cooperation with the Association of Candy Technologists quickly developed and implemented a four-week course in 1967. Thirty food and candy processing managers and technicians took the course, which was supported by fees paid through industry.

—The college offers an in-service training program for dietary aides employed in eighteen municipal hospitals; 320 enrolled. On successful completion of the program, the employees receive an increase in pay and higher-level jobs. A similar program was developed for approximately 1,000 nurse's aides who are being trained as technical specialists, i.e., obstetrical technicians, operating room technicians, inhalation therapists, ambulance technicians.

—Under a $17,850 contract with the Housing and Development Administration, thirty inspectors who will be assigned to Code Enforcement Centers (centralized units for rehabilitation of poverty areas) are being trained in human relations as well as inspection techniques. This program, a by-product of the building inspectors program, will become a part of the $6 million New York Program for revival of borderline communities. HDA is using it as a model for similar programs elsewhere.

Another outstanding example of in-service training programs for business and industry can be found at Del Mar College in Texas. (See Appendix E for description of program.)

Community counseling: Included in this category are educational and vocational guidance and counseling services for those members of the community who are not now and never have been day or evening students of the college. The service is particularly geared to retraining and dropout problems of the community. In addition to individual and group counseling and guidance, services include periodic occupational conferences, widespread testing, special guidance publications, and in-plant counseling and testing.

A most promising community counseling project is underway at Cuyahoga Community College in Ohio. Project SEARCH, a counseling center located off-campus, offers comprehensive educational counseling service to help individuals identify realistic goals for themselves. The boundary for the program is Cleveland, although outlying communities are served. Counseling is aimed specifically at residents of the Hough area, a disadvantaged section of the city.

SEARCH has been in operation since July, 1967. Its establishment was aided by a $60,000 grant under Title III of the Higher Education Act. Clients for the service are recruited through lists of graduates and drop-outs obtained from four high schools that serve the Hough section. Letters describing the Center's services are sent to each former student with an invitation to come in. During the first six weeks 138 people accepted the invitation. The Center seeks to help individuals develop realistic goals for themselves.

Newsletters providing limited information about career opportunities were mailed and telephone calls were made to those on the lists who were personally known to members of the staff. Paid counselor aides visited those who did not respond. These aides are two women from the Hough community who are very close to the people and have served on almost all of the committees that have been organized there. Some recruiting has also been done through newspaper reports of activities. The number of counselees has increased weekly.

Other exemplars in community counseling are the Area Guidance Center operated by North Florida Junior College for six rural counties; and the New York State Guidance Center for Women sponsored by Rockland Community College, New York, in cooperation with the State University of New York. (See Appendix E for a more complete description of their programs.)

Human resource development: As "the vehicle of social change and advance" the community college provides programs to broaden the community's educational base and tap a potential reservoir of knowledge, manpower, and experience. Included are retraining programs; basic education programs for the functionally illiterate; Head-Start, Upward Bound, New Career, Manpower Development and Training Act (MDTA), and short-term occupational and basic skills programs for the disadvantaged; and special programs for the increased leisure of senior citizens and others.

Laney College of the Peralta Junior College District, California, has found an effective means of offering skill-training for the culturally and educationally deprived through its East Bay Skill Center. Funded entirely through the Manpower Development and Training Act, the Skills Center is a massive effort in skill-training for the culturally disadvantaged and the educationally deprived. Instituted in February, 1966, its primary aim is to develop good citizenship and raise mathematics and the communication skills, so that maximum benefit may result from the occupational training. Geared toward the underemployed and the unemployed, the program serves students from all six cities in the Peralta district. During 1967–68, about 1,400 students, adults and youths, were enrolled.

Operation of the basic Skills Center is separate from the rest of the college. Housed in a 500,000 square foot building, its faculty is recruited among persons with experience in working with the culturally deprived. There is no credit for courses and no tuition. Students receive a stipend while attending class. Courses are from twenty to forty-nine weeks. Closed circuit TV and teaching machines are used. Community acceptance of the program has been excellent.

Other outstanding examples of projects designed to develop human resources are the urban center operated by New York City Community College and designed to help prepare high school graduates in the lower quarter of the class for job training and placement; and project SERVE of Oakland Community College, Michigan, which offers free counseling and placement for senior citizens in need of additional income, a volunteer placement bureau to help the community utilize the talents of older people, and short courses tailored to the needs of older citizens. (See Appendix E for more complete descriptions of these programs.)

Campus radio-television station: Several community colleges utilize campus educational FM radio stations and/or television stations in their programs of community services. Colleges participating in this study reported the use of these stations for special programming for public events held on the campus and community development and self-improvement. Colleges operating educational television stations also reported using them for television teaching.

Representative of these colleges is Milwaukee Institute of Technology in Wisconsin, which, in cooperation with the Milwaukee public schools, assists in presenting more than 800 telecasts annually to 70,000 students and teachers in over 130 Milwaukee schools. One channel, a VHF station, presents most of the programs, with a UHF channel serving as a backstop when conflicts occur and also for evening adult courses.

The programs are produced by the Department of Educational Television in the division of curriculum of the public schools. The college provides the engineering staff and director. Study guides, workbooks, etc., are produced by the public schools under the instructional resources department. Guides are produced for the classroom teachers in all subject areas and at all grade levels.

Programs include the areas of mathematics, science, language, history, art, music, physical education, and current events. They provide enrichment, instruction in areas previously limited by personnel and budget, major resource presentations to secondary schools, and programs for the teaching staff. All lessons are planned in cooperation with various supervisory departments, classroom teachers and principals. The videotapes are produced in college facilities or are purchased. Most are produced locally, however, with the public school paying for facilities and the right to broadcast.

Other examples of the use of FM radio stations and/or television stations for community service include the public school radio broadcasts of Long Beach City College; and TV College, operated by Chicago City College. (See Appendix E for more complete descriptions of these programs.)

III. Community Development

Objective area three includes leadership and advisory assistance by college personnel; research and planning; studies, surveys, and polls; workshops, institutes, and conferences; and organization of community councils, coordination councils, and other needed community agencies and groups. Community development, a frequently overlooked community service, may be thought of as the college and community joining together in attacking unsolved problems—the college making available to the community resources of knowledge and skills, but leaving decision-making in local affairs to the citizens (12:14). It is in the area of community development that the community college has its best opportunity to integrate with the community.

Bertis L. Jones has defined community development as finding ways of "helping communities to help themselves through the efforts of their own citizens" (11:17). He lists three essential factors: (1) self-help, (2) grass roots citizen participation, and (3) consideration of the total area of community life.

Leadership and advisory assistance: The community college, recognizing that it must be of and not just in the community, makes available to the community its leadership capabilities in coordinating efforts toward community improvement, the solution of community problems, and the improvement of the functioning of community organizations. In this way the college emphasizes the importance of understanding and cooperation between agencies and organizations, business and services, which are interested in contributing to the total good of the community, and promotes the development of local leadership. Services in this category include stimulation and support of community action projects, leadership training, and technical services to agencies of local government and groups of citizens to make community action more effective.

Abraham Baldwin Agricultural College in Georgia provides an example of active community leadership. Desirous of being a part of and of maximum service to its community, the college initiated Project SURGE (Systematic Utilization of Resources for Growth and Efficiency) for the city of Tifton and Tift County in 1964. This unique organization, of which the college continues to be the sustaining force, is made up of people from all walks of life and every corner of the county who have joined for sound growth.

SURGE, an attempt to encourage individuals and organizations to work together in solving community problems that cannot be handled satisfactorily by one individual or organization, is the outgrowth of a meeting of the president of the college and eight local and state leaders. A second meeting drew sixty community leaders from many different fields to discuss community needs: acquisition of an industrial site, tax revaluation, beautification, improved education, development of a centralized civic and fine arts center, and the like. A later community-wide meeting attracted 300 residents of the county and Operation SURGE was underway.

Fourteen SURGE committees represent every aspect of community life: agriculture, beautification, business, culture, education, finance, government, health, industry, natural resources, organizations, recreation, religion, and youth. A nine-member steering committee chaired by the college president provides leadership and coordination. Each of the fourteen committees has drawn up goals and objectives for five years, to be used by SURGE members as a scorecard on how resources are utilized for growth and efficiency during that period. Many goals have already been achieved: for example, location of new industry in the county; beautification of public property; acquisition of an adequate art gallery and a public library; organization of the governmental planning committee, composed of city commissioners and the city manager, county commissioners, state legislators from Tift County, president of the Chamber of Commerce, and the chairman of Operation SURGE; establishment of a Mental Health Clinic; organization of a school of nursing at the College; organization of a Council of Civic Clubs; and construction of a new youth center and a 10,000-seat football stadium.

SURGE has published a brochure setting forth project aims, and made a thirty-minute film to publicize the program. Committees meet periodically, and the countywide meeting, a kind of town meeting, is held annually. All community organizations belong to SURGE, and in lieu of their regular meeting, hold their official meeting of that month during the SURGE annual meeting.

A short course, "Community Development for Community Leaders," funded under Title I of the Higher Education Act, was developed as an outgrowth of Operation SURGE as a means of studying the role of community leaders, what their duties and responsibilities are, and how they can best serve the city and county.

Studies, surveys, and polls: The importance of understanding the community cannot be overemphasized. In fact, it has been said that the effective community services administrator is one who has an "almost encyclopedic knowledge of his community." The gathering and dissemination of information needed to solve community problems is essential if the community development phase of the program is to meet community needs. Such data can best be acquired through a community survey; other methods include occupational surveys; studies (frequently utilizing college students) and polls.

The value of a comprehensive community survey was demonstrated by Cerritos College in California when it undertook a two-part community survey in cooperation with a citizens advisory committee composed of city managers, chamber of commerce managers, school superintendents, and coordinating council presidents from the college district communities. Part one was a socioeconomic study of the district; part two, an opinion poll with special questions for the several communities in the district.

Results of the survey convinced the college that it should

Greatly increase its program of community services in all areas to satisfy the expressed needs of the people.

Improve communications with the public to keep people informed of events occurring on campus.

Create a Public Forums series emphasizing "name" speakers on political and social issues, and respond to the strong public endorsement of art shows, art workshops, musical concerts, pop music, singers, jazz programs, fine arts films, school dramatic events, and the like.

Initiate, in cooperation with local communities, a comprehensive series of research studies, seminars, conferences, etc., related to current problems and future needs of the communities.

Establish a comprehensive library of information about the district.

Develop an FM radio station.

Undertake a study of the feasibility of a museum.

Have a series of conferences to coordinate the various community agencies dealing with vocational guidance, and plan its own Vocational Guidance Clinic in cooperation with those agencies.

Establish facilities to increase its research activities in both community services and institutional development, and assume the role of "community research center," much as the university does on a state-wide basis.

Continue the following existing programs: (a) Speakers Bureau, (b) Community Use of College Facilities, (c) Summer Recreation Programs.

Open the college library for public use.

Study the needs of business and industry in the area and, on the basis of the information revealed, set up a series of special workshops and seminars designed to solve the needs and problems of various businesses and professional groups.

Workshops, institutes, and conferences: Needed educational resources for community action programs are provided for the purpose of mutual aid and enlightenment through workshops, seminars, institutes, conferences, and the like. Through these services the community college assists in the education of its publics on issues vital to the continuing welfare of local communities.

Essex Community College in the suburbs of Baltimore, Maryland, has developed a dynamic program in the community development field consisting of information and education about local government, planning, renewal, community organization, etc. The college sponsors workshops and seminars especially geared to provide the needed educational background for many action programs.

Some of the features of the unique community development and action programs held during the 1966–67 academic year are

Conference on air and water pollution attended by 200 citizens from all walks of life—city officials, state officials, lay citizens, etc. This program and all others are free.

A four-week action course on local government, at this writing running for the fourth time. This is a noncredit, tuition-free course attracting approximately fifty enrollees each time. Though now offered at the college and in the community, industrial executives are presently negotiating for an in-plant course.

Seminars—notably, the constitutional convention seminar, by which the college became a vehicle for bringing the convention to the people.

A seven-week tuition-free course on the convention, offered on alternate weeks.

Planned for implementation during 1967–68 were

Publication of a community services guide listing all public and private agencies that do things for people.

Holding a four-week public relations conference in four areas of discussion: (a) Public Relations in Advertising, by a public relations firm talking to the civic presidents; (b) Publicity, by a panel of newspapermen; (c) How to Get Members and How to Raise Money, by a national organization; (b) Lobbying Techniques, by a professional lobbyist.

Opening up the campus to a Government Fair Day, where people will have an opportunity to talk with government officials.

Offering a short course (free) in national government and national politics, and a program to coincide with the national conventions.

The community services program, organized in 1966, was funded totally by a Title I grant, and application is being made for a second grant. The director of community services works with an over-all advisory committee for his office, the functions of which are to identify (a) problems, (b) what the college can do to solve them, and (c) what the college can do to help people solve their own problems.

Organization of community councils, coordination councils, and other needed community agencies and groups: The community college makes a significant contribution to its district community by assisting in the establishment, coordination, and sustenance of needed community groups. As a grass roots institution, it is a prime agency for identifying what needs to be done and for supplying the resources with which to achieve satisfaction of needs through local action. Services in this category reported by community colleges include a mutual concerts association, area arts councils, a council of social agencies, a management institute, and a police academy.

An excellent example of college and community joining to meet a community need is found at Rockland Community College, New York. The Management Institute at Rockland Community College, Inc., a self-supporting, nonprofit, educational corporation, is concerned with program planning and diagnostic work for the management community—a service not previously available except through private consultants. The Institute "creates a bridge between industry and the regular college curriculum." Its function is to provide development and training courses in management and supervisory skills for industrial and commercial firms, government agencies, professional personnel, and other organizations in the area.

Founded by area business, civic, and educational leaders, with the support and participation of the New York State School of Industrial and Labor Relations at Cornell University, the Institute is affiliated with and located at the college. Short-term, noncredit training courses and workshops for foremen, supervisors, managers, and professional personnel are offered both on and off campus. In addition, the Institute researches, designs, and conducts in-plant management and supervisory development seminars to meet the special needs of a given organization. The total enrollment of the Institute as of the fall of 1967 was 289, benefiting 118 different organizations.

Other examples in this category are the Area Audio Visual Materials Center organized by North Florida Junior College to serve six counties; and the Oakland Police Academy operated by Oakland Community College, Michigan. (See Appendix E for more complete descriptions of these programs.)

IV. Cultural and Recreational Activities

The fourth objective area of the program of community services includes arts, lectures, and film series; cultural tours and field trips; gallery programs; physical activities; community science services; festivals; and community performing groups.

The community college has an important responsibility in the cultural development of its community and region, and the implicit obligation to contribute toward raising community standards of entertainment and recreation. A cultural center and focal point of the intellectual life of the community, the community college also enhances the value of other cultural and recreational institutions in the community and enables them to extend their services. In this area it is vitally important that the college identify those services already available in the community in order to avoid unnecessary duplication.

Arts, lectures, and film series: Most community colleges offer public events series designed to appeal to members of the community and college students alike. This phase of the community services program is directed toward the community-at-large rather than to smaller specific groups, as in the case of short courses. Included in the public events series are public affairs forums and lectures, usually planned as single appearances of noted personalities with audiences of several hundred; lecture series, symposia, and conferences for smaller groups; concerts, drama, recitals, ballet and modern dance; other cultural events staged for college and community; and classical and art films, museum films, foreign films, historical films, and travelogues and documentaries.

As part of its community services program, the Foothill Junior College District, which operates Foothill College and De Anza College, sponsors an extensive public events program that attracts over 25,000 persons annually, and is designed to meet the needs of both the students and the community. Four cultural series comprise the public events program: Fine Arts, Lectures and Forums, Art Exhibits, and Film.

The program is developed and sponsored by a Public Events Board. The Board is composed of faculty members, day and evening students from both campuses of the college district, and representatives from the District Office of Community Services. Each of the four series is planned by a different student-faculty committee of the Board.

Among program attractions, the Fine Arts Series brings to the community outstanding professional performers in drama, music, and the dance. The Norman Luboff Choir, Swingle Singers, Andrés Segovia, the Moscow Chamber Orchestra, Theodore Bikel, and the Little Angels are some of the well-known artists recently featured in the series. The series attracted some 7,500 persons in 1966–67. Dr. Max Lerner, General Maxwell Taylor, C. Northcote Parkinson, Dr. J. B. Rhine, Carey McWilliams, Cleveland Amory, Pearl Buck, Robert Hutchins, Marquis Childs, Alistair Cooke, and Dr. Erich Fromm have taken part in varied and well-attended groups of forums.

Art exhibits are presented monthly in the college library. Hundreds of art patrons enjoy paintings, photography, lithography, etc., executed by professionals and faculty members.

The Film Series provides cultural enrichment, presenting films of merit that appeal to students and the college community. More than 4,000 adults attended the 1966–67 Film Series program and the Independent Film-Makers Festival. The Festival provides students and the community with an opportunity to see and discuss the best in recent experimental and independent film-making and encourages individual expression and experimentation in this area.

Representative of cultural events staged for smaller groups is the seminar in the arts held in the spring of 1967 by Flint Community Junior College in Michigan. (See Appendix E for a description of this program.)

Cultural tours and field trips: Included here are group visits to places and events of interest to residents of the college district community, such as musical and stage events, art exhibits, museums, historical sites; vacation tours of the U.S. and abroad; and field trips for the purpose of exploring science and the arts.

Flint Community Junior College extends the bounds of the Flint "cultural area" with its Tours and Trips program. The program serves to supplement the rich offerings of Flint's community art, music, and drama organizations with the best available in surrounding areas. It helps to broaden the horizons of local persons to include understanding of other parts of the world and serves a community group no other part of the adult program serves completely. A total of 1,200 to 1,400 participants were served during the 1966–67 academic year by twelve to fifteen short tours, a tour through the Shakespearean Festival at Stratford, Ontario, a Mediterranean Holiday, and the Highlights of Europe. A forty-one day Around-the-World tour has been included in the past. Short tours include offerings in art when the Detroit Museum of Art and the Toledo Museum of Art are visited. The Metropolitan Opera in Detroit and Hill Auditorium in Ann Arbor have been destinations of musical ventures. Drama presentations such as those held at the Fisher Theater in Detroit and Meadowbrook Theater at Oakland University are also included.

Many kinds of people take advantage of the Tours and Trips—older citizens, single women, widows, and others who find the complications arising from making their own arrangements or the problems involved in traveling alone undesirable. Ideas and interests are shared and new friendships are formed.

The trips are figured on an actual-cost basis resulting in a reasonable cost to the individual and encouraging participation. The program is self-supporting.

Gallery: A number of community colleges maintain art galleries or gallery programs for the benefit of both college students and community. Programming includes art exhibits—painting, sculpture, crafts; science exhibits; photography exhibits; and features community exhibits as well as professional travelling shows. Occasionally lecture series are related to the exhibits.

Cerritos College in Los Angeles County, California, is a community college that operates an art gallery. In 1966–67 the college hosted 26,000 people at its Art Gallery. Financed through the Office of Community Services, the Gallery houses approximately twelve shows per year, with every effort being made to exhibit work that has wide appeal to the community as well as application to the art instructional program of the college.

Four of the exhibits each year are usually standard traveling art rentals obtained from various museums and galleries throughout the country. There is a community art show with collections made through the various community art associations and judged by area professionals. Fine Arts Associates, a community services citizens advisory committee, has representatives from each of these art associations and sponsors the shows. It also sponsors a high school art competition each year with work on display from the fourteen high schools served by the college.

In addition, the Cerritos "Invitational" and Cerritos "Open" are scheduled each year to bring contemporary professional art to the community and the student body. The "Invitational" exhibits the work of two area artists who have shown unusual ability and/or secured a reputation for good quality contemporary art. Any work of art may be submitted for prejudging by a neutral agency for showing in the "Open."

Controversy over the shows is kept to a minimum by studied diversity and careful balance of faculty and lay advisory committees. The Gallery director is a member of the college art faculty and is assisted by a part-time Gallery assistant who works on crating, shipping, and mounting art pieces.

Physical activities: The community college also contributes to the health and physical well-being of the members of the community through community recreation programs. These physical activities are planned and supervised by the college and include skills classes, tournaments, track and field events, weight conditioning, clinics, special events, and nonorganized free-time activities.

Cerritos College has also developed an imaginative summer recreation program, which fits the needs of the entire family. The activities fall into the categories of aquatics, fine arts, and sports, and are staged throughout the college district. Planning and scheduling of these cosponsored activities is shared by personnel from all recreation agencies and school districts in the Cerritos College District. Administrative heads of these various recreation agencies form the community services recreation committee, which meets monthly to plan the programs and solve common problems related to recreation. During the summer of 1967 over 110,000 persons participated in a recreation program. The total program was designed for the entire family. More than 45,000 people participated in the aquatics program alone. Swimming instruction was given to more than 16,000 children.

In the fine arts area such activities as art workshops, junior and senior music camps, creative, social and square dancing, and dramatics were included. Nearly 35,000 people participated in these events.

A varied sports program attracted some 31,000. Included in the activities were sports leagues, baseball, basketball, archery, gymnasium free play, track and field all-comers meet, weight training, and wrestling.

The Cerritos program supplemented those of the recreation agencies in the district, taking advantage of the personnel, facilities, and equipment available at the college. A recreation program is provided during the school year also, again in cooperation with the in-district recreation agencies.

Community science services: A number of community colleges operate planetariums, observatories, and science museums as a part of their programs of community services. Lecture-demonstrations are provided on an organized basis for elementary school classes, high school groups, special community groups, and the adult community. Occasionally, distinguished men of science are presented as visiting lecturers in connection with planetarium or observatory programs. Professional organizations and societies are sometimes encouraged to affiliate with the local community college.

Foothill College houses a growing Space Science Center. Now in operation are a planetarium, observatory, Project OSCAR (Orbital Satellite Carrying Amateur Radio), and "Operation Moonblink." The Peninsula Astronomical Society, comprising fifty students, engineers, and technicians, utilizes Space Science Center facilities. Members of the Amateur Research Center, sixty high school and college students and technicians, are affiliated with the Center.

The Planetarium provides a popular program for area fifth and sixth graders as well as adults. In 1967–68 daily lecture-demonstrations drew 21,000 school children and 5,300 adults. Eighty-nine different elementary schools participated in the school program, with the school year booked solidly through May. Evening and Sunday programs are offered for the public.

Following the evening Planetarium program, the Observatory is open to the public. More than 5,300 persons participate annually in evening demonstrations there. The Observatory is also a key unit in the international network of twelve observatories participating in the NASA Argus Moonblink Program. The name, "Moonblink," is derived from the technique employed in observing certain luminescent phenomena on the sunlit surface of the moon.

Project OSCAR is an example of cooperation with individuals and industry to foster significant developments in science. The OSCAR Association has created a complete tracking station and communications center in its temporary quarters on the campus. Peninsula radio amateurs have financed and built, to date, four satellites, which have been carried aloft aboard research and development vehicles of the U.S. Air Force. Through an OSCAR receiver, transmitter, and amplifier, as many as twenty two-way communications have operated simultaneously and messages been relayed as far away as 6,000 miles on its international two-meter ham band.

Ground has been broken for an electronics museum to house an historical artifact and document collection that was donated to the college district. Over 2,000 items in this outstanding collection trace the history of electronics since the turn of the century. Some $200,000 for construction of the museum has been donated by local industries. At its completion, the museum will be administered by the college with the private foundation that donated the electronics collection acting in an advisory capacity.

Also planned as part of the complete Space Science Center are a thirty-foot radio telescope, linear accelerator, electronics laboratories, telescope-making laboratories, a mathematics-computer science center, and a technical library. Laboratory opportunities for elementary school children, special activities for high school and college students, and group research projects for community adults will be provided.

Festivals: Festivals of the arts include fine arts, music, drama, and ballet. Festivals are usually staged for both college students and community during the summer months or academic year. Occasionally, the community college joins with community groups in the sponsorship of a community wide festival of the arts.

Cabrillo College in California, jointly with the Cabrillo Guild of Music, stages a highly successful annual Music Festival during two weekends in late August with ten concerts scheduled. Since its inauguration in 1963, attendance has escalated each year, passing 5,000 in 1966. The festival is also a financial success. Income is derived from a vigorous fund drive, ticket sales, special donations, and program advertising and has climbed to an annual figure in excess of $27,000. While costs run nearly this high, a small balance is maintained.

Press coverage is excellent, releases and notices being carried in such distant publications as *Opera Canada* and *The New York Times* as well as in local newspapers. A festival brochure has been printed with the cost of the 20,000 copies being paid by the Greater Santa Cruz Chamber of Commerce. In addition, the Santa Cruz County Advertising Committee provides financial assistance in advertising outside the county and ticket orders come in from greater distances.

The entire festival is recorded for broadcast in prime time on a nearby radio station and videotapes are made for twelve hour-long programs in San Francisco and Salt Lake City.

Orchestra members, most from the Bay area, with several from southern California and others from Washington, Iowa, Virginia, New York, and other areas, are offered accommodations in many homes throughout the county. They perform an outstanding series of concerts at the end of a very few days' work under the brilliant coordination of a conductor and two assistants. With the exception of a few students, all members of the orchestra are professionals.

Community performing groups: This category includes choral groups composed of members of the community as opposed to college students, community orchestras composed primarily of community personnel, and community theater groups under the supervision of the community college. The community choruses and orchestras are organized around the principle of rehearsal, performance, and education. Performances are scheduled on a year-round basis. Community theater groups, however, perform more frequently during the summer months and present a wide selection of plays and musicals for children and adults.

One of the more outstanding examples of community performing groups in the music field can be seen at Del Mar College in Texas, which has become a cultural center for its college district. The college has organized four community performing groups in music: The forty-five member Del Mar Chamber Orchestra, the eighty-voice Corpus Christi Chorale, a more select, thirty-voice Schola Cantorum; and the Corpus Christi Symphony Orchestra, which has now become an independent organization.

The Del Mar Chamber Orchestra, organized to provide an outlet for professional calibre musicians in the community, is presently composed of college students, faculty, and community people. Begun as a group performing strictly for pleasure, the community performers will be paid in the future for the five or six public concerts per year, which are given in the college auditorium or recital hall.

The community symphonic choir, the Corpus Christi Chorale, attracts 1,000 to 1,200 persons to each of its two or three annual performances, which are directed to the listening pleasure of "the musically discerning audience in the community." The group, selected by open audition, rehearses two hours weekly for the two or more major choral works it performs with orchestras each year.

The Schola Cantorum is composed of professionally trained singers in the community. This ensemble is devoted to the study and performance of musical literature suitable for chamber chorale groups. The college provides the choral director and rehearsal hall, to which people come from the surrounding towns one night a week to prepare for three performances given during the year. In 1968-69 a performance was given in Mexico City with the National Symphony Orchestra, all expenses for the trip being paid by the college.

While the Corpus Christi Symphony Orchestra was originally founded by the college and received all of its financial support from the college during its first eight years, it is now an independent organization with a separate governing board. The college continues its support, however, by providing free rehearsal space and a minimum charge for concerts, free box office service, and by underwriting a percentage of the salaries of faculty members and students who perform in the orchestra.

A fine example of summer theater programs can be found at Flint Community Junior College, Michigan. (See Appendix E for description of program.)

Taken together, the foregoing examples would seem to substantiate the destiny of the American community college forecast by Tyrus Hillway some ten years ago: ". . . the true community college becomes an integral part of the social and intellectual life of its locality. Through lectures, musical programs, community surveys, informal study groups, cooperation with employers and placement agencies, donation of its facilities for civic functions, and a hundred similar methods, the institution raises the cultural, social, and economic level of its town or district" (9:80).

SELECTED REFERENCES

1. Basler, Roosevelt, "Consistent and Increasing Adaptability of the Junior College," *Junior College Journal* XXV (April 1955).

2. Bogue, Jesse P., *The Community College*. New York: McGraw-Hill, 1950.

3. CJCA Committee on Community Services, "Summary of Community Services Questionnaire for California Junior College Districts." Unpublished report based on study of fifty-one junior college districts. California Junior College Association, Sacramento, Calif.: 1967.

4. Gould, Samuel B., "Whose Goals for Higher Education?" Remarks prepared for delivery before 50th Annual Meeting, American Council on Education, Washington, D.C., October 12, 1967.

5. Harlacher, Ervin L., *A Study of the Community Services Function in California Public Junior Colleges*. Norwalk, Calif.: Cerritos College, April 1964.

6. Harlacher, Ervin L., "California's Community Renaissance," *Junior College Journal* XXXIV (May 1964).

7. Harlacher, Ervin L., *Effective Junior College Programs of Community Services: Rationale, Guidelines, Practices,* Occasional Report No. 10, Junior College Leadership Program. Los Angeles: School of Education, University of California, Los Angeles, 1967.

8. Henry, Nelson B., ed., *The Public Junior College*. 55th Yearbook, National Society for the Study of Education. Chicago, Ill.: The University Press, 1956.

9. Hillway, Tyrus, *The American Two-Year College*. New York: Harper & Brothers, 1958.

10. Johnson, B. Lamar, *Starting a Community Junior College*. Washington, D.C.: American Association of Junior Colleges, 1964.

11. Jones, Bertis L., *The History of Community Development in American Universities With Particular Reference to Four Selected Institutions.* Unpublished Ed.D. dissertation, University of California, Los Angeles, 1961.

12. Lackey, Katherine, *Community Development Through University Extension*. Carbondale, Ill.: Southern Illinois University, 1960.

13. Medsker, Leland L., *The Junior College: Progress and Prospect*. New York: McGraw-Hill, 1960.

14. Menefee, Audrey G., "There's a Meeting Here Tonight," *Junior College Journal* XXXI (March 1961).

15. Price, Hugh G., *California Public Junior Colleges*. Bulletin of the California State Department of Education, SSVII, No. 1 (Sacramento, Calif.: The Department, 1958).

16. Reynolds, James W., "Community Services," in Nelson B. Henry, ed., *The Public Junior College*, National Society for the Study of Education, 55th Yearbook, Part II (Chicago, Ill.: The University of Chicago Press, 1956).

17. Sheats, Paul, Clarence D. Jayne, and Ralph B. Spence, *Adult Education*. New York: The Dryden Press, 1953.

18. Vines, Eugene T., *Community Service Programs in Selected Public Junior Colleges*. Unpublished Ed.D. dissertation, George Peabody College for Teachers, 1960.

19. Woods, Thomas E., "Community Development—3rd Phase of the Junior College Movement," *Junior College Journal* XXVII (September 1956).

A
Major
Function
Still
Emerging

3

Despite its growing acceptance as a major function and repeated urgings for strengthened programs, community service is still an emerging function of the community college. Audible and written support for the community services program tends to outstrip the number of visible, constructive local programs.

"The colleges that are the furthest along in working with their communities," according to Ralph Fields, "are less advanced in this regard than they are in other services such as preparing young people for [senior] college or a vocation" (1:81). Depending upon the viewpoint of the college concerned, there appears to be a tendency to exalt or denigrate the community service function to suit the point of view. If the institution is committed to the philosophy of the community college itself—namely, that all persons, regardless of age or educational background, are welcome to enter its open door—then the community services function assumes a position of importance equal to that of the other four community college functions. On the other hand, if the transfer function is the primary concern of the college, the community services program indeed may be treated as a stepchild.

One reason for the slow emergence of community services as a major function is the fact that many presidents, deans, other administrators, and faculty frequently regard the program of community services as secondary, an amplification of the standard functions, not as a separate function.

This secondary role can be seen in the way the program of community services is administered in the community college. Studies and surveys by several authors during the past eight years, including one by this author of fifteen independent junior college districts in California, have shown that even where a wide array of services was being provided, the program of community services was still not being administered as a major function equal to the transfer, occupational, and counseling and guidance functions. Today, this continues to be a problem.

The community college's basic inferiority complex is another factor retarding the development of community service as a major function. Still in the process of becoming an accepted institution, and "uncertain and insecure of its place among other educational institutions," the community college lacks the "courage to be different" and looks to the four-year institution for a model. To obtain needed prestige, this dynamic new institution allows itself to become hidebound by restrictions, traditions, and a sophistication more in character with the four-year college (6:1).

Coolie Verner has challenged the community college to ". . . identify and capitalize on its unique role and construct a program, design an organizational structure, and employ methodology to fulfill that role rather than being content to remain an inadequate copy of patterns designed for other roles and other functions answering different needs" (6:6).

MAJOR PROBLEMS AND ISSUES

Administrators of community colleges included in this survey reported that they are faced with problems of varying degrees of magnitude in the development of effective programs of community services. These fall into eight broad categories of administrative responsibility: (1) internal and external communications; (2) securing the support of boards of trustees, the administration, and faculty for community services; (3) coordination of service with other community and regional groups; (4) identification of community needs and interests; (5) planning and evaluation of the program; (6) development of a program philosophy and identification of objectives; (7) administration and supervision of the program; (8) adequate resources. Each problem category will be examined in the following discussion.

I. Internal and External Communications

Effective internal and external communications involve many facets of community and college life. Within the college, it is necessary that channels of communication between the community services office and other college offices involved in providing services be clear cut, so that confusion and duplication of effort can be avoided. Outside the college, it is essential that a wide variety of media be used to reach all segments of the college district community. Internal communications can be regulated and strengthened at their source; it is the effectiveness of external communications that is of vital importance to the growth of the entire college, both in stature and in service.

The president of an Illinois college, expressing his conception of the philosophy of the community college, has perhaps pinpointed the cause of many problems associated with communicating successfully with the public. "The community college," he says, "represents a newness in education. It is a new breath, a new hope, and a new try at making a local educational institution a real and vital part of the community of people who support it." This very "newness," this "new try," may engender suspicion, or, at very least, caution among the people the college is trying to reach. For people are frequently resistant to any attempt to exchange the unknown or the new for the known and familiar, no matter how ill suited the latter may be for meeting their needs. Such was the consensus of a number of respondents in this survey, particularly in reference to their attempts to reach the people of the inner cities.

"It seems that communities who need the most help are the most difficult in which to develop enthusiasm," observed a representative of a California community college, speaking of the educationally and culturally disadvantaged. How to engender interest in participating in programs specifically designed for them is a problem with which the colleges will increasingly be faced, especially those in the larger urban communities, according to a number of interviewees. For in the ghettos, the people— inured to drudgery and distress, to unemployment and unkept promises politically inspired and bureaucratically buried—have learned to substitute apathy and suspicion for interest and enthusiasm.

This assertion is borne out by the statement of an Ohio community college official who deplored the fact that means of communication, effective with the socioeconomic strata characteristic of the outer community, are useless in the inner city. "These people lack information on what's available," he said, "but the problem is how to give it to them. Communication is critical. To send out brochures, evening schedules, and so on, just doesn't do the job." There must be some means devised by which to reach these people, perhaps by going out into the community on a one-to-one basis or in the company of someone who is known and respected in the inner city. But such an approach involves the expenditure of much time, both in "selling" the program and in "human engineering." The colleges are not in a position to do this by themselves; they must have the cooperation of interested organizations in the total community.

The advantages to the community college of encouraging participation by citizen groups in activities designed to promote the welfare of the college and to reveal the needs and aspirations of the community, or any segment of it, are obvious. If the over-all program of community services is to achieve the highest degree of success, it cannot be constructed from the college point of view alone. Without benefit of counsel from interested community representatives, such a viewpoint could easily place greater emphasis upon theoretical considerations than practical requirements and fail in its purpose because it neglected to take into account the needs that can only be made known by members of the community itself.

Lack of understanding of community services, however, is not confined to the inner cities. It extends throughout some communities. As pointed out by an Arkansas interviewee, many people do not associate community services programs with college. Nor do they recognize the community college as an agency that is available to help, a New York administrator adds. This results from perpetuation of the college stereotype—college is a complex of buildings housing students who are preparing to enter the professions. Thus, the most pressing problem in a number of communities is how to educate people to the community college philosophy and the services available. Too often communities become actively aware of their colleges only when painfully reminded by requests for community approval of bond issues or tax overrides. In overcoming this obvious handicap to good college-community relations, a wide variety of information services provided by the college for its district community can prove to be invaluable. An excellent example of this was supplied by a Virginia administrator who described a special section that interpreted the college's program in a local metropolitan newspaper. The articles and photographs for the special section, prepared by the institution's public information office, brought a new point of view to many citizens who formerly had regarded the community college as "off limits" to any but those engaged in formal education.

Another approach, a rather unique one, was suggested by a California administrator who was having similar problems in external communication. Relating military strategy to the development of community services programs, he pointed out: "You don't attack a territory all at one time; you establish beachheads, and through them have control." In his view, a very real problem is the college's taking the initiative in attempting to acquaint the total community with its extra-classroom services. He suggests working through other organizations and groups. "These local organizations are geographic islands, cultural islands, and they serve the constituency of that section of the community. The selling is done by the 'natural representative' and not the college."

This approach might well deserve the consideration of community services directors, particularly those in newly established community colleges. New institutions offering new services face the difficult problem of securing community identification with the college. As an administrator in a new Pennsylvania college pointed out, "Many segments of the community are unfamiliar with the college itself, let alone what possibility exists in the way of community service programs."

To overcome this particular handicap, a California community college developed a citizens advisory committee of seventy-five community leaders for the sole purpose of communication. Members of this continuing committee meet semiannually on the campus to discuss such topics as purposes and objectives of the college, vocational-technical programs, current status of the college district, selected curriculum areas, and community services. Each member constitutes an individual "wave-length" that can be tuned in by the citizens within his sending radius so that, in the aggregate, the committee has contributed much toward community awareness of the college itself and of the services it offers.

A Wisconsin college has another surefire method of effective college-community identification. It requires that each short course offered be cosponsored by a community organization. Although no pressure is put upon the organization, in many instances it pays the fee for speakers and frequently provides its own mailing list for the sending out of flyers, occasionally furnishing the postage as well. In such circumstances, it is difficult for the community long to remain unaware of its college. Stimulating interest where apathy prevails, educating the public to the community college philosophy, promoting the program of community services, making all members of the community aware of the college offerings, developing the community's sense of "oneness" with the college—all of these are problems that cannot permanently be solved. They can be alleviated, using means suggested earlier and others that become self-revealed in time, but communications will require continuing attention.

II. Trustee, Administration, and Faculty Support

The importance of having board, administration, and faculty support for the community services program can hardly be overemphasized. When, as in one college, the board is "dedicated to making the college truly a community institution," the community services administrator's battle is already half won. But, as happened in another college, when there is need to "educate trustees to the fact that community services contribute significantly to public support when crucial issues are presented to the electorate," this attitude is likely to filter down through the administration and the faculty and so place the program in jeopardy. This is not to say that indifference—even opposition—to the program always originates with the board; far from it. Many community college educators themselves do not accept the community services concept, regarding it as a "watering-down" of the more formal academic offerings. This position reflects a failure on the part of the college personnel to understand the unique multipurposed role of the community college. A need therefore exists in some institutions to orient the faculty and staff to the concept that, without community services, the college is not a community college.

As one Maryland interviewee put it: "Essentially, the faculty are concerned that noncredit courses and services may not be fully college level and that they therefore detract from their preferred image of academic transfer preparation." And a New York administrator added that the faculty is apathetic toward "facing problems outside its own discipline."

The concern of the community college, therefore, would seem to be for finding means of reconciling the striving of the faculty for personal prestige as "college instructors" with the larger purpose of serving all members of the community. The narrow view that community services are of secondary importance to the regular academic program prompted one administrator to exclaim, "But we can't just sit back on our comfortable swivel chairs while the community goes to hell!" Nevertheless, this is what too many colleges may be forced to do if they allow their faculties to continue rejecting the community services program as a major function of the community college. Faculties and, in a number of instances, administrators as well need to understand the appropriateness of ways of training other than through college credit programs. One Texas interviewee, himself committed to the principle that "a community college ought not to be concerned about being collegiate—it ought to be concerned about being a community service agency," put the matter this way: "There is a mistaken fear on the part of boards and chief administrators that, if they offer services on too broad a basis, they will depreciate the regular college program. When community services are considered, they raise the question, 'Is this really collegiate?' They fear the college will be blighted by what they regard as substandard. The community gets to feeling this way about it, too, and this feeling is reflected in the elected board. The board sees its chief responsibility as one of helping youth take their place in life. Some members even take the position that they should not use tax money to rescue the derelict. It's a case of perpetuating the great American dream—the guy who gets the Ph.D. or the M.D. and goes on to fame and fortune with everyone claiming the product. No one is concerned about the adult who has been upgraded through one of the community services programs."

Many community services programs have been developed grudgingly for their public relations value. That they do have public relations value, both faculty and administrators are willing to concede; but they continue to regard these programs as a segment of activity possibly better placed outside the jurisdiction of the total institution. Indeed, one administrator suggested the appropriateness of establishing a separate institute with corporate status to sponsor community services programs. The principal reason for this suggestion was to make it possible for controversial issues to be considered. A California interviewee explained that the closeness of the community college to the community for support presented a critical issue, for it is "politically difficult for the college to air controversial issues." This was a view expressed repeatedly by interviewees in all parts of the country, and in New York, for example, an institute was established as a separate corporation with a separate board, although it is housed on the campus, so that it could be protected from the politics of the local board of trustees.

This "need" to be protected from self-serving faculties on the one hand and from political pressure groups on the other places the community services function in a position somewhat analogous to that of the illegitimate son at the family picnic. Although it serves a broader purpose than formally educating students for transfer or work; although it reaches into every corner of the community and therefore has high public relations value; and although it must play a secondary role at all levels and in all areas in many institutions that call themselves "community colleges," the program apparently has much yet to do to justify itself as the fifth major function of the community college.

An administrator in a Washington college, commenting that "we must break through the traditional mind of the educator to enable him to see the fantastic potential of the community services program," nevertheless explained why this is difficult to do. "Probably our most significant problem," he remarked in connection with his own institution, "involves teaching migrant workers to read Spanish, in order to teach them how to read English. They are illiterate often in both languages and must be started reading (interpreting symbols) in the language of greatest facility. From this point on, it's a process of getting them to the various 'equivalent' levels. This is most difficult for the academic faculty to understand as a legitimate function of a college."

Another problem is the potential community criticism of the community services program of any large size. One California interviewee was particularly disturbed, because he believed that such criticism might trigger a revolt against the restricted community services tax funds provided by state law. He was of the opinion, however, that adverse community feeling was probably fostered by faculty unsympathetic to the community services concept. The interviewee expressed the gravity of the situation in these words. "In my judgment, the special community services tax rate in California junior colleges will lose its preferential position unless considerable work is done in the near future to broaden the basis of understanding among faculty. It will be in the educational house itself where the most serious objections will be raised about the continuance of this tax."

Faculty and community services personnel do not always work at cross purposes, however. Another California administrator reported the serious efforts of his college to broaden the image of community services. Commenting on the "lonesomeness of the community services office," he reported concentrating during the current year upon improving its image. And a Pennsylvania college was able to report that its board of trustees has a basic policy that would make the college a catalytic force in the community. The college thus is encouraged to be of service to all segments of the community—to industry and the culturally disadvantaged alike, and to secondary and elementary schools. It is likewise urged to do some probing into causes of dropouts, so that it may assist in retaining high school students to high school graduation. "If the only concern of the staff is with maintaining their status as college teachers in the academic or occupational programs, no one is aware of it. In this college, the community services program is *not* the low man on the totem pole!"

III. Coordination of Services with
Other Community and Regional Groups

One of the major purposes of the community services program is taking the college to the community by encouraging college staffs to participate in community affairs. Faculty resources involve consulting, research, and speakers as well as the provision of college leadership in finding solutions to community problems—especially college action in the cultural field. Provision of these services, however, engenders certain problems for the college, particularly when activities overlap or duplicate services already being provided by other community and regional groups. When this occurs, the college is placed in the unfavorable position of competing with other agencies and institutions.

One Florida community college faces an unusually difficult situation in this regard. Located in a county whose school system operates a very large noncredit program in its evening high schools, a center for technical education, and one for general education, the college finds its own offerings in constant conflict with those of the county. Moreover, a nearby private four-year college has recently appointed a director of continuing education whose primary responsibility is the promotion of noncredit courses, while a regional state university not far away duplicates many of the community college's services through the eleven specialists on its continuing education staff. The result has been that the community services function of the community college has largely been assumed by those other institutions. "The citizens are surfeited with educational offerings," the spokesman for the college stated, "yet there is so much more that really ought to be done, particularly in reaching professional and special vocational needs." Such proliferation without coordination reduces the services of all agencies to mere competitive scrambles for enrollments. It does not service the community; it only confuses it.

A similar but even more distressing problem is faced by a California community college, which is located within a 25-mile radius of twenty-two four-year colleges and eight junior colleges, and surrounded by five high schools that offer adult programs. All of these institutions offer typical lecture, film, art, music, short courses, conferences, etc., programs; and most of these programs overlap or duplicate each other. The problem is further confounded by the fact that the district board of trustees takes the view that the regular academic and occupational programs are the primary concern of the college, and that community services constitute little more than unnecessary furbelows. Moreover, the board has rejected all appeals for a study to determine just what the college should be doing for the community-at-large.

The importance of close liaison and cooperation with public school personnel and other community and regional groups to avoid duplication of services and conflicts of interests would seem to be self-evident. Yet the difficulty of assigning responsibility for individual offerings remains unresolved. In this connection, according to a Missouri interviewee, the community college must take the initiative by getting the directors of the different programs together and effecting a working relationship that will not encroach upon respective areas of jurisdiction. But this is easier said than done in most instances, and the problem grows more acute with each passing year. In some communities, for example, the senior college has revived the concept of taking the leadership in community development and, often with the superior attitude assumed by the older brother toward the younger, has tended to discount the efforts of the junior college. Where the two can work in cooperation, however, the results are salutary for both. A private senior and a public junior college in a Texas community, for instance, recognizing the overlap of programs offered, made a cooperative study of community needs and the institution best suited to meet them. The senior college, which currently offers an extensive noncredit program, conceding that its efforts can be applied more effectively to the activities ordinarily characteristic of four-year colleges, now plans to phase out its community services program and allow the junior college to assume full responsibility. But this kind of cooperation is usually the exception rather than the rule.

Perhaps a better solution to the problem of uncoordinated services with the community, according to a California interviewee, would be the development of regional planning or statewide master planning of community services efforts. In support of his argument, he cited several abortive attempts by his institution to undertake cooperative projects involving the university, the state college, and the community college. "These have failed, in my judgment," he stated, "because of the lack of some sort of central agency to coordinate and administer the projects." If a statewide master plan were established, in his view, the architect of community services would have a blueprint to follow in developing his program, safe in the knowledge that he was not encroaching upon the province of any other institution. However, with the exception of state plans for Title I of the Higher Education Act of 1965, required by federal law, few states have developed any plan for coordination even remotely resembling a master plan for community services.

In the absence of such a statewide blueprint, the organization of communitywide coordinating councils might provide the mechanism by which to avoid or at least minimize conflict between community services offered by the community college and those offered by other community groups and institutions. The organization of such councils will, of course, depend upon the extent to which the college is able to involve the community in planning and development, and this involvement, in turn, will depend upon the college's ability to identify community needs and interests. Some of the problems attendant upon this latter activity are discussed in the following section.

IV. Identification of Community Needs and Interests

Involving the community in planning and development includes the utilization of community groups, individuals, and community leaders in the planning and promotion of the program of community services; the cosponsorship of services and activities by appropriate community organizations; the use of community advisory committees; and the organization of a community advisory council to assist college officials in identifying needed community services. The decision to provide a specific service cannot be based upon the hunches of college staff members alone; it must be grounded in an analysis of the community's needs and interests. Such an analysis can best be made after a community survey, and with the insight provided by conferences and discussions with community people. Once the college has taken the initiative in this regard, the community-at-large ought to be encouraged to bring specific requests for services to the college.

All the foregoing is well and good in theory; in practice, it is not always operative. As a representative of a Maryland community college observed, "Too often we take the attitude that the college knows best what the people need." This attitude, unfortunately, precludes either identifying the community's needs and interests or attempting to meet and fulfill them. And, in some instances, this is justified on the ground that "the people don't know what's good for them." As remarked by the same representative just quoted, "Our community services administrator says he always smiles when we say that we meet the needs of the community, for the community is not aware of its needs." Such a statement appears to be rather too sweeping to be accepted at face value.

People *are* aware of their needs, as the experience of a Florida community college proved. In a "man-in-the-street" type of survey, the college sought to determine the public's reaction both to its community services program and to the college in general. The survey was conducted from September through November 1966, and interviews were held in office, homes, stores, as well as on the street. The candid responses of some 250 people from all walks of life were so revealing that the community services program for the ensuing year was revised to meet more adequately the needs and interests expressed.

Recognizing the value of identifying community needs, a California community college administrator suggested that this be done through closer contact with civic and cultural groups and through a study of the makeup of the community—ethnic, religious, educational, occupational, etc. Such a study was part of a comprehensive community survey used by another California community college as a base for the establishment of a diversified program of community services. And a new Virginia community college reported a "major study in progress to determine where we are going."

While agreeing that community needs and interests must first be identified if the community services program is to reach every segment of the community, a California administrator warned against being wholly governed by community demand. There must be a "happy medium," in his view, because the college, through long experience in developing teaching curricula, is well equipped to help people determine discriminately which of several needs and/or interests can be fulfilled with greatest advantage to them. "We all use, or should be using, committee systems to reflect the opinions and desires of the community; and we would presume that these committee systems are set up in a manner to reflect accurately the composition of the local population. Yet, notwithstanding this impeccable procedure, *how many times can one listen to Louis Armstrong?* At the committee level there must be a very subtle kind of leadership by the community services administrator to urge the committee to be experimental and innovative."

In exercising this "subtle kind of leadership," the community services administrator must also be aware of the danger that identified needs may not be real needs, and that the program he and his colleagues devise may not satisfy the actual community requirements. "I think," said an administrator of a Pennsylvania college that serves a broad area, "the major problem here is a matter of choice—choice of what kinds of programs are really appropriate to this particular institution in this locality." Pointing out that his college endeavors to supply programs that are both experimental and innovative, he nevertheless observed, "We don't know whether they actually succeed in meeting basic community needs or not. If we confine ourselves to community surveys, we may get superficial responses to questionnaires which indicate certain needs to the college administration and faculty, and still leave hidden needs beyond their vision." This, of course, is a problem for which there is no ready solution. The only hopeful approach to a solution, according to a Michigan administrator, is to "secure maximum community involvement on both an individual and organizational basis."

Discovering needs and interests through community involvement may come about in several ways. A Georgia community college, for example, has used advisory committees for the purpose most successfully. Annual meetings of advisory committees—of which there are ten—are held as an all-day session in May. The committees represent every phase of community life—farming, home economics, business, finance, cultural pursuits, and the like—and their membership includes leaders in each respective field. Since these people are leaders, they are in close contact with the citizens of the college district and thus able to communicate to the college the needs and interests expressed to them.

Advisory committees can and should be the eyes and the ears of the college in identifying community needs and interests. Acting on this principle, a California community college organized for this purpose an advisory committee composed of city managers, chamber of commerce managers, school superintendents, and coordinating-council presidents from the college district area. This committee was highly successful in making known to the college *all* community needs and desires, and in assisting the college to chart a course calculated to meet or satisfy them.

The foregoing examples illustrate what has been done—what *can* be done—by way of identifying community needs and interests. They do not, however, provide a solution to the main problem; namely, how to identify the *real* needs and interests of the community. But they do suggest ways and means by which these real needs and interests may be brought to light. Community services administrators must always be mindful of the fact that their programs, however carefully constructed, will fail unless they can discover real needs and real ways of meeting them. The problem in this area lies not so much in identifying transitory requirements as it does in being able to pinpoint those needs and interests the meeting of which will lift the general populace to a new level of fulfillment and/or understanding.

V. Planning and Evaluation

Fulfillment and understanding must be of permanent quality. Neither can be tossed off, like so many hot cakes on a griddle, to be consumed and forgotten until the next pangs of hunger strike. Both require the nourishment of a diet, scientifically sound and constitutionally accurate, if they are to survive the placebos that sometimes find their way into burgeoning programs of community services.

Unfortunately, as one Florida interviewee pointed out, any expressed need or interest often triggers the launching of a program, whether or not it has long-range value. "The offerings grow like Topsy, because the community is so hungry there is no time to develop a quality program." As a result, the college staff becomes so busily involved that it cannot properly evaluate its offerings. "There is no organized approach to the problem," said another administrator, "no long- or short-range planning." In consequence, programs are initiated imprudently in the hope that they will "catch on." If they do not, they may be continued, hopefully, on the grounds that they are merely "sleepers" awaiting proper recognition. Either course can be costly, both to the college and to the community-at-large or those segments of it with special needs.

There can be little doubt that long-range planning of the over-all program and detailed planning of specific services and activities are imperative if colleges are to avoid maneuvering themselves into unproductive situations. And this planning must be conducive to staff experimentation and innovation in developing the program.

If the program is to escape being patterned, as a Michigan administrator suggested, "after high school adult education arts and crafts programs," planning for it must begin at an early date. Special consideration ought to be given to such apparently insignificant matters as provision of on-campus parking facilities or bus accommodations from areas poorly serviced by public transportation and to the timing of events. If the timing of an event is poor, if some detail is overlooked, or if plans are hastily drawn, the program can easily be a failure. In one community college, the time selected to hold an open house was during a season when members of the community were preoccupied with their own affairs; in another, the time of the event was changed at the last minute.

When possible, the services and activities should be related to the instructional program for maximum benefit to students as well as the community, and participants should be encouraged to evaluate the effectiveness of the services. However, as a New York administrator pointed out, "No matter how well you plan ahead, how to get sufficient support from the community to help fulfill its identified needs remains a problem."

This observation suggests the desirability of following two courses: (1) involving as many people as possible in the planning of programs—not merely community groups and individuals, but students and faculty as well; (2) tailoring the program to meet the needs of specific groups rather than the community-at-large. Administrators almost universally cite the importance of organizing a student-faculty committee to assist in planning the community services program, of establishing faculty study and advisory committees, and of encouraging both students and faculty to participate actively in the program. A Florida community college, for example, utilizes a student-faculty-community board in the development of its annual artists series.

Involving the community in the planning and development of the program of community services can be a highly effective procedure. Not only do community groups provide valuable suggestions for program development, they can also be counted on to promote community interest and support. One college, for example, was able to obtain cosponsorship of its recreation program by the city recreation department; in three other instances, citizens' advisory committees, composed of representatives of college district recreation agencies, were formed for the purpose of coordinating the multitude of separate recreation programs in the college district. When a New York community college relied too heavily upon assistance from a community organization in promoting an event, however, both the event and the college suffered.

Other effective procedures include careful preplanning of all advisory committee meetings and encouraging community groups to utilize college facilities and resources. A California administrator described asking representatives of all cultural organizations of the college district to a meeting at which time they were invited to "make their home on the college campus." This resulted in the college becoming the cultural center of the community.

These procedures serve not only to bring together divergent points of view but also to orient intramural personnel to the community services function. So far as catering for specific groups is concerned, this tends to hold the program within manageable boundaries and to facilitate participants' evaluation of offerings in selected areas of group interest.

Adherence to these guiding principles will not eliminate all problems relating to either the planning or the evaluation process, particularly where bureaucratic attitudes and academic inflexibility continually put community services on trial; it can only serve to minimize them.

VI. Philosophy and Objectives of Program

Eventually, one must come to grips with the fundamental elements that go into the building of programs of community services. In the first place, what does *community services* really mean? There was little unanimity of opinion in this regard among the individuals interviewed during the survey, although there was general agreement that *community services* is the broadest of the three terms: *community services, adult education,* and *continuing education.*

A California administrator commented on the failure of traditional adult education and formalized evening college programs to meet the needs of the vast majority of the adult population of local communities: "Adult education is still pragmatically oriented (how to do it). We offer foreign language, for example, so that people can go to a foreign country and speak with the natives. We use the same static approach by instructors, inculcating encyclopedic information; same evaluation procedures over and over again."

Evening college classes aren't the answer for these people either, he continued. "The community college evening classes have moved almost exclusively in the direction of traditional degree programs or training in certificate programs. The great masses of citizens have progressed to the point where they have no need for degrees or they have two or three degrees already, but still lack education. These busy people can't commit themselves to seventeen Tuesday nights with mid-terms and finals; they are not interested in credits."

Professional people will just not submit themselves to "the undergraduate treatment—knowledge for knowledge's sake," according to the California community services administrator. "These people are looking for an educational program which will make a real difference in their lives— an integrating force to help them put the pieces of the puzzle together; they are searching for self realization. An important aim of the program of community services," he concludes, "is to open up new avenues of human growth and movement through an interdisciplinary approach, so that the individual can begin again or accelerate the process of constantly becoming."

The lack of agreement on definitions is also reflected in the objectives of the program of community services. If this were not so, there would be more positive agreement concerning the scope of services to be rendered. One administrator, for example, narrowly conceived of the program as being "limited to nonstructured cultural, fine arts, and social action programs." On the other hand, another interviewee, frankly critical, observed: "There is a tendency for community colleges to ignore some of the social, economic, and political problems in the areas they serve. It is obviously much more comfortable to deal with the conventional—for example, cultural activities, community groups, and so on. With only a few exceptions, community colleges have not been an effective force in working with and solving critical problems of urban areas." Still another blamed lack of administrative leadership for the poor—or at least uneven— development of programs of community services. "Up to now," he commented, "we have been hung up on viewing community services as essentially cultural programs and intellectually oriented forums and lectures."

Another problem, equally vexing, grows out of the danger that community colleges will emphasize the public relations value, rather than develop a sound, philosophical base and a clearly thought-out set of objectives for community services programs. "The spreading of the efforts of the college over a thin layer of highly visible but superficial community activities may be good for short-range public relations purposes," said one Pennsylvania critic. "But such shallowness will inevitably return to haunt the institution in the future."

This point of view was supported by an administrator of a California junior college district whose two community colleges have already taken aggressive steps to activate an effective outreach program in their district: "The major issue facing the district in terms of its over-all community services program is in the area of the long-range philosophy underlying this aspect of the college's function. For too long community services have been interpreted rather narrowly as those programs primarily cultural in nature presented by the college for the educated and culturally sophisticated segment of the community." Attributing this attitude largely to the support given it by "middle-class administrators and faculty," he went on to say: "What this district has embarked upon as a result of [an] investigation connected with [its] inner-city project is a re-evaluation and eventually a restatement of the aims and purposes of the total community services programs at both colleges with the view in mind of incorporating into its program a far wider range of cultural, educational, and recreational experiences for the disadvantaged . . ." of the inner cities.

Another interviewee stated: "I am simply suggesting here that, euphonious though the terminology may be, it is my opinion that few colleges have developed community service programs of any depth or significance."

Such a view cannot be taken lightly, especially since it is voiced by one involved in the program, although it seems to be rather severe in light of the exemplars reported in the preceding chapter. But any attempt to gloss over the fact that many colleges do provide only "highly visible but superficial community activities" would be unrealistic. The chief problem here appears to have its roots in the different concepts surrounding the objectives of community services programs. These seem to have become entangled with the objectives of adult and/or continuing education and educational public relations, and to imply the need for careful differentiation and definition of community services provided by the community college.

Essentially, the formulation of a restatement of the aims and purposes of the total community services program is a major need in most of the community colleges visited in the course of this survey. It seems clear that, before organizing and administering the program, and before soliciting community support for it, its philosophy and objectives must be stated in terms that cover every aspect of its endeavors. It is one thing to offer a program, stereotyped by predecision at the college level; it is quite another to offer one that has perennial appeal for widely differing audiences. Although it is difficult to determine the distribution of program emphasis, it is probably unwise to stress any one facet to the adumbration of the others. Just where the emphasis will be placed, of course, depends primarily upon established philosophy and program objectives.

VII. Administration and Supervision

The problems attendant upon finding knowledgeable and creative administration and upon, as a Maryland administrator put it, "founding programs and the understaffing, underfunding, and understatusing them" are related to the establishment of a realistic philosophy and set of objectives for the program, emphasized in the preceding section. In the present and succeeding sections, the ramifications of these and other problems are developed more fully.

Leland Medsker has said that the extent and effectiveness of programs of community services are related to the administrative leadership they receive. The requirements for the program listed by Medsker include centralized direction, time, energy, money, and adaptability to change as desired types of services adjust to changing community patterns (3:79). These requirements were reemphasized time and again during the course of this survey. Many besieging difficulties would be obviated, it was believed, if responsibility were centralized in a single administrator, whose staff and budget were sufficient to provide the necessary freedom and support for developing a strong program. It was also emphasized, however, that if he is to exercise effective leadership for this important function of the community college, the community services administrator should be relieved of other duties such as evening college responsibility, teaching, administration of student personnel or the instructional program, or having charge of an academic division. No administrator whose responsibilities and energies are unduly divided among multifarious duties can perform any of them with maximum efficiency. Among other things the community services administrator ought to be free to spend a certain amount of time in off-campus field work, not only in working with community groups in the interests of college-community cooperation but in "spotting" areas of need among those segments of the population unable to identify these for themselves. It was the general consensus that if he is bogged down in intramural responsibilities, related only secondarily to community services, such activities will be restricted, if not impossible.

And according to James Reynolds, "the personality of the administrator may be one of the most important factors which facilitates or inhibits the development of . . . community [services] programs" (4:34).

But, asked a Texas administrator practically, "Where would you go to get a good community services man? There is a distinct lack of leadership training. Even the Kellogg Leadership Program doesn't prepare men for this kind of assignment." A California administrator agreed that finding "knowledgeable and creative administrators appears to me to be a real problem." And an Indiana administrator stated that "the major problem in the development of a program of community services is finding people with talent and public relations skill, as well as specialized skills, who can work with community groups." The laments of these community college administrators over the lack of leadership training programs for community services administrators is well founded. With the exception of traditional adult education leadership training programs offered by schools of education in a few leading universities, there is a leadership training void.

What are the qualifications of the community services administrator? While there is not universal agreement on the job description, community college leaders emphasize that the most effective administrator of these programs is one who possesses

1. Sufficient educational background to be able to work with the college staff in a major administrative position, including course work in the community college.
   (At least one postgraduate degree would be required unless the person had considerable experience as an educational administrator.)
2. Professional experience in community service, community development, community action, community relations, university extension, and/or adult education programs.
3. Ability to work with other leaders of all types.
   (Telling people what they need is no sure method of interesting them in acquiring it. A great deal of tact and human relations skill are needed if the potential service of the college is to be realized.)
4. Knowledge of the college community or of the various communities within the district or service area.
   (This is not the same type of knowledge that same phrase would have implied five to ten years ago. Today this means familiarity with political forces, with the concerns of differing ethnic and economic groups and subgroups. It means having some degree of knowledge of the agencies already serving these communities and of the gaps in that service.)

Certainly a list of minimum qualifications for an effective administrator of community services would include a comprehensive understanding of and commitment to the unique role of the community college in society and firsthand experience in community service or related work.

A California interviewee suggested that current organizational patterns in community colleges would likely discourage a qualified man from assuming a post in which he would also be assigned other duties considered "more important," thereby restricting any innovative abilities he might possess and confining him to the role of minor college administrator. Centralized leadership, therefore, must carry with it the connotation of exclusive province—not merely added responsibility. Unfortunately, as another interviewee pointed out, in most current situations it is extremely difficult to hold men with leadership ability as directors of community services. This results, at least in part, from the "understanding" of the community services program. "Good men tend to move up the ladder," a Texas administrator complained, "to accept more prestigious administrative positions. They felt frustrated by the lack of commitment to the program on the part of boards and presidents, and stymied by the fact that they are attempting to rear a child whose origin many regard as illegitimate. Those who stay in the community services positions are the least creative, the least imaginative. These are the ones who 'top out' in community services."

And yet, as a Wisconsin administrator observed, when the director of community services is given equal status with other administrators, as his was, and placed in a position of influence in policy development, the desire to move "onward and upward" dies aborning. "The success of our program," he remarked with understandable pride, "is directly attributable to the unique vision and leadership of our director, including his ability to plan and organize." In essence, the program of community services, in direct distinction to a more formalized curriculum, must constantly change, experiment, innovate. It must be dynamic to be successful. This was the opinion of a California interviewee, who also suggested that attaining this goal is, in large part, dependent upon the employment of a full-time community services director.

Internal blocks, however, frequently make it difficult if not impossible for the program of community services to retain its dynamic quality, even with a full-time director. Many colleges do not allow sufficient flexibility for this unique program. Too often such services get caught up in the regular program; i.e., credentials are required, the college is overly concerned about accreditation requirements, the college curriculum committee must act on all of the programs, division chairmen must be assured of the academic quality of the community services program. And the services become college rather than community oriented. A new Maryland community services administrator, for example, reported getting his wrists slapped for violating a rule by registering students for a short course in the classroom.

Thus entangled in internal procedures, those concerned with community services must find ways of combatting "the establishment" and its point of view that if an offering receives no credit, the college cannot support it; that, certainly, if it is less than a semester in length, the college cannot regard it as important; and if it utilizes a medium other than the classroom it will depreciate the "regular program."

The community services director, besides being given a free hand to develop the program, must also have adequate staffing of his office if effective community services are to be rendered. Obviously, he cannot perform all the necessary duties by himself. Recognizing this fact, a few colleges have provided support staffs including full-time assistants for community education, community development, and cultural affairs; a full-time supervisor of civic center services; a full-time auditorium manager; a full-time professional manager for the campus radio and/or television station; a recreation coordination enthusiast, well-qualified staff coordinators for the program with freedom and authority to develop their activities; and an adequate number of clerical assistants. This kind of foresight and insight on the part of college boards and presidents, unhappily, is evident in too few instances. As a result, many community services programs are required to limp along from goal to goal in the fervent hope that they will not collapse entirely before the next goal is reached.

The problem is compounded, according to a Washington State community services administrator, when college policy dictates drafting regular faculty to serve in the community services program. Faculty members frequently are unenthusiastic about such assignments—particularly when no provision is made for compensation. And a related difficulty, according to the same administrator, involves identifying and drafting qualified part-time instructors from noncollege sources, since these individuals often must be approved by the college curriculum committee and/or personnel division. Such required approval, whether or not denied, does little to enhance college-community relations and frequently deprives the community services program of experientially qualified personnel. This is not to say that the community services director should be permitted to operate outside established college policy; it is only to suggest that sufficient preplanning be carried out to determine in what areas he may act autonomously.

An adequate full-time staff means sufficient personnel with enough time allotted to organize and expedite services and activities included in the program. It means staff coordinators, selected on the basis of their qualifications and enthusiasm for the program, provided with the necessary time and authority to plan and coordinate their activities, and with adequate clerical assistance. It means enough people to provide expert staff help for citizens' committees selected to represent all segments and views in the college district community. "Some community colleges," a Wisconsin administrator pointed out, "are located in geographic isolation. They're built in affluent sections of the community." He cites the need to use off-campus centers. Such centers cannot be serviced, however, until the college provides representation where they are. This is a major responsibility of the community services director and his staff, a responsibility that gives promise of growing as the years increase.

All of the problems discussed in this section thus far were familiar to interviewees in small and large districts alike. One problem, however, is unique to the larger, multicampus districts. As a Missouri interviewee put it, "The question of how to administer community services in a multicampus district is a real poser. Should the program be administered from the central district level, or should there be a decentralized administration on each campus of the district?" The answer to this query probably lies partially in the development of a college district master plan for community services as well as the state master plan suggested earlier. Certainly, the need for centralized coordination of community services programs in multicampus districts was apparent to a majority of administrators in such districts. "It is my hope," commented a California administrator, "that the design of any district master plan will ensure that the program of community services is developed on a districtwide basis. In my judgment, there should be a district community services office to develop and coordinate the total program." And a Wisconsin college representative stressed "the significance of centralized leadership for the program in order to maintain a single image for the multicampus college."

In the final analysis the question of how to administer the program of community services in a multicampus district is one which must be decided by the local district. However, that decision ought to be based on a careful analysis of the objectives of the program of community services and the audiences(s) to be served. It would be incorrect to assume at the outset that just because the decision had been made to administer the formalized curriculum (schooling) offered for youth and adults from 8 a.m. to 10 p.m. at the campus level in a decentralized fashion, that the same decision would automatically hold for the program of community services with a different set of objectives and an entirely different audience.

Certain requirements for and characteristics of the program of community services ought to be considered in reaching a decision regarding the program's administration in multicampus districts.

—The concept of the community dimension suggests that the community college meets the needs of its district community through two different educational programs, formal and informal education. This allows the entire college district to be a campus for the program of community services and permits a "metropolitan type government" rather than a piecemeal attack upon the multifarious educational, economic, social, and cultural problems of the total community.

—The ideal locale for a program of community services, according to Maurice Seay and Ferris Crawford, is one "in which there are numerous communities with natural and compelling interrelationships" (5:144). The program of community services welds these separate communities and groups together.

—Most community college districts meet the criteria for community and thus are rather ideal loci for programs of community services: (a) area with common sources of information; (b) natural and geographic area; (c) area in which people perform their economic activities; (d) area in which people find their normal recreation; and (e) area with natural or common ethnic groups.

—Community development work requires a regional approach, if community problems are to be solved, and stresses mobility and coordination.

—The program of community services is community oriented rather than college or campus oriented. The program is planned to meet the needs of citizens who are not now, nor may ever be, enrolled in formalized classes on the college campus. It must not become a public relations tool for the local campus.

—To avoid unnecessary duplication of services in the community, the program of community services must be carefully and continuously coordinated with other community and regional groups.

—The program of community services is an outreach program, which utilizes campus facilities in conjunction with many other community facilities in taking the program to every corner of the college district.

—The program of community services must remain flexible and dynamic and cannot afford to become caught up in the structure created for the other major college functions.

—An effective program of community services requires the employment of specialists in such areas as community education, community development, cultural and recreational affairs, rather than additional general administrators.

—An effective program of community services is based upon a carefully developed philosophy and set of objectives that have been tailored to meet the needs of the college district community.

The foregoing characteristics again suggest the need for a districtwide master plan for community services. It seems abundantly clear that regardless of how the program is administered, all district services for the community, many of which admittedly duplicate or overlap those of other community organizations and institutions, must be drawn into some sort of pattern compatible with the over-all philosophy and general objectives of the program of community services.

VIII. Resources

But however well conceived a district community services master plan may be, where and how to secure sufficient funding for the program is a problem that looms large for most community services administrators. According to E. T. Vines, "The success of the program seems to be determined largely by the viewpoints of the administrators and their ability to organize available resources" (7:245).

Inclusion of the community services function in federal programs for community development and human resource training and retraining has made some federal funds available, but most districts are yet to benefit from this kind of financing. Those that do often find the allotments earmarked for specific purposes connected with the general welfare of the nation and require mountains of paperwork.

In a few states—Maryland, Michigan, New York, Ohio—Title I of the Higher Education Act of 1965 has had a profound effect on the establishment by community colleges of imaginative community services. Other states, however—including California and Illinois—report that community colleges have difficulty competing with four-year colleges and universities for these funds which are earmarked for community services. "No junior college application has been approved up to the present time," an official of the Illinois Junior College Board reported.

During the course of this survey, little state aid for community services was seen throughout the country, and there was little evidence to suggest that this situation would change much in the immediate future. Since state apportionments are based upon enrollments or average daily attendance, any help from this source, as presently structured, would force a class format for the program that is unsuitable for many of its purposes.

The only alternative has been to require that these programs and services be self-supporting, with success often measured in terms of the amount of money made. The objection to this requirement, according to an Arkansas administrator, is that it eliminates some of the people who would otherwise be served. "The programs are most extensive," he remarked, "in colleges where they are free or a very small fee is charged." Even so, certain difficulties are involved in the free or small-fee programs. One of these, a Washington community college representative explained, is subsidizing programs to enable the college to set a fee interested participants will pay. And so far as free services are concerned, the over-all program is frequently placed in jeopardy because of the need to siphon funds away from the rest of the program for the community services program, which most colleges are unwilling to do. In this connection, a Texas interviewee pointed out, "There is a trend toward curtailment of free programs as we move into a tighter economy, because the college administration takes the position that if they have to charge for the program, they won't have one at all."

Another problem involves the lack of seed money. "The program can't pay its way in the beginning," commented a Maryland administrator, "yet the administration feels that if we can't meet our expenses in the community services program, we had better forget it." One of his colleagues added, "We are required to submit a profit and loss statement to the business office in advance for every activity we propose to offer." He added with feeling, "The business manager should not dictate the educational program of the college." Neither should the regular staff be permitted to retard the community services program. Although taking no overt action to do so, according to a Florida interviewee, the staff "sometimes throws a passive monkey wrench into the works." While supportive in theory, staff members may not in fact offer equal support in use of facilities, personnel back-up, and realistic financial support. "Community services cannot become an integral part of the total college offering," he went on, "as long as they must be one hundred percent self-supporting and can only be scheduled and staffed in the gaps left by regular 'day/degree' programs." This sentiment was echoed by many individuals.

Sufficient financial support, besides alleviating the need for adequate facilities and equipment (e.g., the construction of auditoriums and/or little theaters, to cite probably the most expensive), also makes possible the compensation of faculty for certain community service responsibilities. Suggestions specifically cited compensating faculty members for their work in connection with short courses, recreation activities, campus radio and television stations, community counseling, and consulting services. In those instances where such compensation had been provided, faculty participation in the program had accelerated to the benefit of both college and community.

There was general consensus that credit programs take preference in facilities as well as budgets, a fact which reemphasizes the "stepchild" role of community services in many colleges. But, a representative of a Michigan college pointed out, none of these problems would exist if community services were considered a major function of the community college. As it is, he explained, "when enrollment drops off the community services budget is also cut, even though more facilities may now be freed for the program of community services." When such cuts occur, or when budget requests are denied, the community services division is deprived of money for honorariums and other expenses to support the level of programs needed, according to a Florida interviewee, who added ruefully, "This is especially hard to swallow, because income from community services class fees, which should be plowed back into support for new programs, is not."

A somewhat different kind of difficulty was reported by a California administrator who, fortunately, suffers very little from the problems just discussed. "Our problem," he stated, "is to make what we've got extend over ever-widening demands for additional services, and not to be trapped in fixed obligations so that there will be something left over for creative development of new programs of value that we do not yet see or see only dimly."

This Californian does not share the same financial concerns of community services administrators in other states. California, uniquely among the fifty states, in addition to state support for adult education classes, permits a local district maintaining a community college to increase its maximum tax rate by five cents per $100 of assessed valuation for community services purposes; this is done simply by a majority vote of the local board of trustees. One California community college district reported that its income from the community service tax during the last fiscal year was just under $500,000; almost 70 percent of the money, however, was used for capital outlay purposes such as new auditorium facilities. The diversion of community funds to capital outlay projects not directly related to the program of community services, i.e., swimming pools, athletic fields, and general purpose facilities, is one of the major reasons given for recent attempts by the California Legislature to eliminate the restricted tax.

Assembly bills, introduced in the 1965, 1966, and 1967 Legislatures, would have eliminated most tax overrides, including the restricted community services tax. Through efforts of the California Junior College Association's Committee on Community Services, amendments were made to these bills providing for the continuance of the community services tax. However, the matter was not permanently disposed of, as evidenced by the almost annual reintroduction of the measure, and is of grave concern to California community services administrators.

Commenting on this problem, one administrator said: "In all likelihood, we will see by 1969 the elimination of this restricted tax as a result of general California property tax reform. Without the restricted tax, the program of community services will be forced to compete with general fund expenditures, and it is my hope that by 1969, most junior colleges in the state will have a firm enough program to compete vigorously for the available funds."

Another Californian, whose college district encompasses a broad and relatively sparsely settled territory, regretted that all the people of the district community could not be served because "in some remote areas only a few people want a course, and the number is not sufficient to underwrite a class." "Problems" of this kind, it is submitted, most community services administrators could bear!

From the overwhelming majority of reports gathered during this survey, finding money to finance the program remains the chief concern in the area of physical resources. One administrator even wondered, "Will the programs continue without federal funds?" But a counter query might well be: "Will the programs continue if colleges persist in assigning them low priority with respect not only to funds but to staff and status as well?" Looking toward the future, it seems unwise to build too hopefully on the possible availability of federal funds, except on a short-range basis. A more permanent solution would appear to be the inclusion—with peer priority regarding staff, funds, and status—of community services among the major functions of all institutions that claim to be community colleges: (1) transfer, (2) terminal, (3) guidance, (4) general education, (5) community services. But until communities, college faculties, and college administrations can be educated to the fact that semester-long, credit courses are not the only—nor, indeed, necessarily the best—means of bringing enlightenment to the community-at-large, the problems and issues delineated in this chapter will doubtless be but slowly resolved. This is not to suggest that no solutions will be forthcoming; it is only to imply the need for continued and painstaking effort to discover them. *Empta dolore docet experientia.*

CRITICAL REQUIREMENTS

The foregoing problems and issues reported by community college administrators are directly related to the critical requirements for effective programs of community services identified by this author in an earlier nationwide survey of ninety-nine community colleges that claim community services as a major function (2:37–76). Developed from identified behaviors that contributed to or interfered with the success of established programs of community services, these requirements fall into three broad areas of administrative concern: securing community-college support for the program, determining the nature and scope of the program, and organizing and administering the program.

These basic procedures for the effective administration and supervision of the program of community services in the community college are presented in check list form in Appendix D. This check list is offered as a guide for community colleges interested in establishing or strengthening a program of community services.

SELECTED REFERENCES

1. Fields, Ralph R., *The Community College Movement*. New York: McGraw-Hill Book Company, 1962.
2. Harlacher, Ervin L., *Effective Junior College Programs of Community Services: Rationale, Guidelines, Practices*, Occasional Report No. 10, Junior College Leadership Program. Los Angeles: School of Education, University of California, Los Angeles, 1967.
3. Medsker, Leland, *The Junior College: Progress and Prospect*. New York: McGraw-Hill Book Company, 1960.
4. Reynolds, James W., *An Analysis of Community Service Programs of Junior Colleges*. Washington, D.C.: U.S. Office of Education, 1960.
5. Seay, Maurice F., and Ferris N. Crawford, *The Community School and Community Self-Improvement*. Lansing, Mich.: Clair L. Taylor, Superintendent of Public Instruction, 1954.
6. Verner, Coolie, "The Junior College as a Social Institution." *Community Services in the Community Junior Colleges*. Proceedings of the Annual Florida Junior College Conference. Tallahassee, Fla.: State Department of Education, September, 1960.
7. Vines, Eugene T., *Community Service Programs in Selected Public Junior Colleges*. Unpublished Ed.D. dissertation. George Peabody College for Teachers, Nashville, Tenn., 1960.

What's
Past
Is
Prologue

4

The community college is becoming a dynamic force that affects the thought processes, habits, economic status, and social interaction of people from every walk of life in every part of the country. More and more it is emerging as the most compelling element in this nation's educational structure. And this is just the beginning, for a new community college is being built in this country each week of the year.

If what is past is indeed prologue, it seems inevitable that the community college will place even greater emphasis on its community dimension in the decades ahead. The community college will demonstrate, to an extent even greater than it has to date, that college is where the people are, and that community services are designed to take the college program out into the community as well as bring the community to the college.

Moreover, in implementing its full community services function, the community college will break, once and for all, the lockstep of tradition, i.e., college is four walls; college is semester-length courses; college is credit; college is culturally and educationally elite. The community college does not accept the traditional definition of higher education set forth when the University of Berlin was founded less than 200 years ago:

... a society of teachers and students existing not one for the other but both for the sake of scholarship; a society sufficiently insulated from the world to be able to live according to its own inner logic; whose members seek intellectual solitude and are given the freedom without having to participate, to criticize without having to reform (1).

For the community college is dedicated to the proposition that, important as are formalized curricula offered for youth and adults within its classrooms, informal education, provided on a continuous basis throughout the community for all of the rest of the people, is of equal importance in building the character of the citizens who make up the state.

Education, today, is a continuous and total process requiring both formal and informal experiences. Prior to the present generation it was possible for a person to attend a system of formalized education during his youth and learn enough about the nature of man and his environment and develop sufficient personal and civic competence to last him during his lifetime. This is no longer true. He must continually return to school, or have school come to him, in order for him to keep up with the "new knowledge."

No longer can educators sit passively and react belatedly to the pressures of educating the "masses," "unwashed," or "downtrodden," "disadvantaged" or whatever the fashionable term seems to be at the moment. The times are ripe for the impatient to bypass an educational process that has no relevance. "America, whether it likes it or not, cannot sell its social conscience to the highest bidder. It must build new institutions of democratic planning which can make the uneconomic, commercially wasteful and humane decisions about education and urban living which this society so desperately needs" (5:46).

If a major concern today is to increase the capacity of the individual to learn throughout life, then an entirely different attitude is needed toward buildings and conditions under which learning can best take place. The community college campus, as traditionally defined, is essentially "vertical." It is "stacked" somewhere in the district or service area where those *who can*, transport themselves and partake of its services. Higher education has been "vertical" since ancient Roman days, the formality and rigidity of these structures fly in the face of change. Higher education today, especially community college education, needs to be horizontal.

Through its community dimension, then, the community college can provide opportunities for raising the cultural level of the citizens, betterment of occupational status, development of community leadership, and an educational climate in which the citizen can develop his potential.

SEVEN MAJOR TRENDS

At least seven directions which this major emphasis on the community dimension will take seem safe to predict at this point. On the pages that follow, each trend will be discussed briefly and illustrated with anecdotes collected from community colleges through the country.

Multiservice Outreach Programs

1. *The community college will develop aggressive multiservice outreach programs designed to truly extend its campus throughout the entire college district.*

Through the use of extension centers, empty stores, portable units located on vacant land, mobile units, churches, schools, libraries, museums, art galleries, places of business, other community facilities, the community college will establish communication links with all segments of the college district community, encouraging a free exchange of ideas and resources. The community college, stable, yet unfettered by the permanence of buildings, will become a viable force in the community, moving its physical location in response to shifting needs. This flexibility should substitute initiative for withdrawal, allowing educators to blend the world of thought with the world of action in a meaningful way.

In its most significant role, the program of community services constitutes what might be called "Operation Outreach." Peter S. Mousolite has suggested that, "We emulate the English Minstrel, the French Jongleur, the Spanish Trovador, the Chautauqua enterprise so popular not so many years ago," and through the use of mobile units bring library resources and other educational opportunities to the heart of the ghetto (9). The exploding body of knowledge cannot be *walled in* by tradition if it is to be transmitted effectively. Outreach Centers, by joining all segments of the college community to the college and to each other will foster communication: community dialogue; and dialogue for a community college is mandatory. The community college cannot be isolated and inaccessible, whether physically or by attitude.

Commenting on community dialogue, Robert Hutchins said that he used to think that human problems could be treated like scientific problems—"you got the facts, you tested your hypothesis against the facts, and then you had the only possible answer." This "simple-minded carry-over from science," he continued, has done more to retard the development of the human race in the last hundred years than anything else. "I have come to believe that as far as human problems are concerned, the important point is the community, the communal attack on problems, the communication among people. The kind of civilization you're trying to achieve is a civilization of the dialogue. . ." (7).

Spreading informal education throughout the community and making maximum utilization of community physical and human resources will make it possible for education to become, in fact as well as theory, a continuing element in life, essential to effective community living and the personal growth of its citizens, rather than a super element.

English architect Cedric Price, suggesting that education be treated less as a polite cathedral/town amenity, has proposed a 20,000 student campus in North Staffordshire, England, which is built around the local and national communications (road, rail, and air) network, emphasizes temporary housing, and ties students to the community. His Thinkbelt, which encompasses an area of about 100 square miles, will be oriented toward science and technology and will be designed to help the entire community realize that "education at this level is not merely desirable but essential." It will exploit modern electronic communication systems and equipment and make use of mobile and variable physical enclosures (railway carriage lecture rooms, for instance) (10).

Extension centers: A number of community colleges offer college credit and noncredit courses in off-campus extension centers.

Pasadena City College in California conducts noncredit short courses, lectures, and forums for members of the community in sixty-five different sites in every part of the six unified school districts that make up the college district. Tuition-free and given both day and evening, these offerings range in difficulty from a beginning course for those who cannot read to sophisticated classes in electronic computing, management, and supervisory training. Representative of this program is the short course for the wives of prisoners, offered in cooperation with the local Council of Churches. Five sections of the course convene from 9:00 a.m. to 12:00 noon, Monday through Friday, at a neighborhood center, taught by two teachers—one a specialist in homemaking and the other a specialist in parent education.

Another example of extension center programs is the Parent Education Preschool Observation classes conducted by Pasadena City College at twenty-one different locations. Mothers and preschool children attend their neighborhood class once a week. A nursery school program and setting is offered the children. This program for the child provides a "laboratory" setting in which the mother makes a written observation of her child in a group situation, noting growth, and determining norms and individual differences.

The seminar, "Working with the Mentally Retarded," offered by Foothill College in California is likewise exemplary of noncredit courses offered in the community. The six-session seminar cosponsored by seven community agencies was designed to present a detailed description of the physical, intellectual, and psychological characteristics of the mentally retarded child and adult. The short course included visits to one of the cosponsoring agencies for participants who were not currently working directly with the retarded.

Oakland Community College in Michigan illustrates the trend toward offering college credit extension courses in community facilities. Approximately sixty-eight different college credit courses are offered in eight different locations in the 900 square mile community college district. Course offerings include English, sociology, political science, psychology, and economics. Average enrollment for the year is more than 1,200. Noncredit short courses are also offered in off-campus locations.

Similarly, California's Los Rios Junior College District provides district residents with the opportunity to earn college credit in their own communities. The district, which covers 2,600 square miles extending from Lake Tahoe on the east to Napa County on the west, places particular emphasis on extending more community services to the outlying areas located away from the three- or four-mile influence of the district's two colleges, American River and Sacramento City. About forty miles from American River Junior College, the district has developed a satellite campus at Placerville, where more than 270 students were enrolled in college credit courses in thirty-five academic subjects during the fall semester. Also under consideration is the use of closed-circuit television between campuses and especially to those areas which are thirty to forty miles away from the nearest campus. And, in addition to educational programs, the district is exploring ways of taking cultural programs which local campuses enjoy to these communities which seldom have such opportunities. Recently, for example, it took "Shakespeare in the Park" to an open-air stage in Placerville, and was rewarded for its efforts by maximum attendance.

The concept of home discussion groups is a feature of the highly publicized Community Education Project at San Bernardino Valley College in California. It was conceived in 1952 as a special effort to involve greater numbers of people in the study and improvement of the communities in the college district. The project sponsored workshops and seminars, week-end residential conferences, and round tables as well as home discussion groups. These were all designed around neighborhood community and area problems.

St. Petersburg Junior College in Florida has continued the home discussion group concept. The discussion groups satisfy common needs of people in all walks of life for informal, semimonthly evening meetings in private homes where they can propose and discuss topics, electing their own moderator to keep participation interesting. The purposes of the home discussion groups, which average from twelve to fifteen persons, are to explore ideas with others and to broaden one's interest in the friendly and informal atmosphere of the home where there is freedom from classroom or other formal atmosphere. Topics include, "How Would You Improve Education?" "Does Technology Determine Our Way of Life?" and "Looking Into Abstract Art and the Modern Artist." There are no fees for participation. One member commented, "I've been waiting for years to look over ideas I think are important. These people talk just as in a bull session. We get down to fundamentals and as a result learn from each other."

In-plant training: Miami-Dade Junior College in Florida, El Centro College in Texas, Cuyahoga Community College in Ohio, and New York City Community College in Brooklyn are excellent examples of community colleges with extensive in-plant training programs.

Miami-Dade Junior College offers an extensive program of in-plant in-service training. Both credit and noncredit courses have been taught in the County Sheriff's Department, the City Police Department, and in a power plant overhaul company, and noncredit short courses have been given in two airline companies. Noncredit courses have been offered in the South Miami Fire Department, at the post office, in local hospitals, in public schools for lunchroom managers, and in government agencies. Approximately four to five thousand employees in Dade County have gone through the in-service training program and some 1,800 city supervisors have participated in a noncredit course in supervision. These in-service training courses are frequently attended on company time with tuition being partially or fully paid by the company.

El Centro College also offers in-plant courses in fire stations, hotels, insurance companies, savings and loan companies, hospitals, etc. The top management training courses conducted for St. Paul Hospital in Dallas are an example of this program. Three different courses, basic management, work simplification, and problem solving and goal setting are offered for hospital supervisors. The college began the training program in 1966 at the request of the hospital, after securing the services of five top industrial engineers from Texas Instruments, Inc. The work simplification course was given to personnel who previously had completed the basic management course under the hospital's own training program and according to the hospital, the application of industrial management techniques saved the hospital $750,000 in operating costs during the first year. The emphasis upon finding more efficient, less expensive ways of doing jobs resulted in cost-cutting projects in such departments as laundry, food service, housekeeping, etc. The college believes that much of the success of the program stemmed from the hospital administration's endorsement without reservation of the philosophies taught.

As another example of in-plant training, Cuyahoga Community College is planning an in-service training program for federal employees working in the Federal Building in Cleveland. It is estimated that the program would initially attract more than 500 persons, the employees being excused at approximately 4:30 p.m. for the training and the federal government picking up the tab for their tuition.

Mobile and portable units: An increasing number of community colleges are utilizing or considering the use of mobile units and portable facilities to take the college to the four corners of the college district. Oakland Community College in Michigan, and Hudson Valley Community College in New York illustrate this trend.

In an effort to combat the multiple problems of the ghettos and establish effective channels of communication between the ghetto residents and the outer community, Oakland Community College proposes to establish multiservice outreach operations in slum areas—Think-Links between the values of the dominant culture and those of the ghetto subculture. Such Think-Links would form a triangle of strength and community stability to result in understanding. Emphasis would be placed on concrete programs of action rather than elaborate edifices of concrete and mortar. The use of empty stores and mobile units located on urban renewal land would minimize the cost and maximize the flexibility of the program. Features include (1) learning laboratories with programmed materials and multi-media for acquisition of literary and basic skills, (2) community-student action corps composed of leaders from grass roots communities and college students (75% poverty areas), (3) two comprehensive educational and vocational counseling hubs, (4) multifaceted cultural and educational activities, and (5) volunteer faculty and community consulting service.

With a similar purpose in mind but a somewhat different *modus operandi*, Hudson Valley Community College began operating mobile recruiting vans for its Urban Center as a pilot project during August of 1967. Planning for the venture took most of July, culminating in a meeting of over 100 representatives of social, religious, and neighborhood agencies in the Albany area. The "Opportunity Van" began operating from 2:00 p.m. to 8:00 p.m. in two disadvantaged sections of Albany, spending several days in a row in the same neighborhood. Manning the van were administrative personnel, student services personnel and teachers from the Albany Urban Center, and representatives from the New York State Employment Service. The method of operation called for the van to be parked in the middle of a block and teams of two individuals to cover the area, going from house to house knocking on doors and approaching individuals in the street. Each individual was urged to visit the van where his particular situation could be discussed at greater depth. The "Opportunity Van" functioned on seven different days in the two sections. During this period, the staff knocked on 524 doors and spoke to 439 people. Of these, 187 indicated an interest in enrolling in the Urban Center Program, and 162 actually showed up the first day of school. At the end of the first three weeks of the fall term, all but two were still in the program.

Another activity of Oakland Community College, again employing mobile units, is the community science outreach program, which is being developed in cooperation with a local institute of science. Featuring mobile exhibits and demonstrations, traveling museums, and science short courses, the program is being designed to permeate every corner of the college district. Projected are scientific exhibits and demonstrations to be transported to store fronts in disadvantaged areas, portable buildings on vacant lots and urban renewal land, community schools, and other centers throughout the county. Traveling museums are to be parked in strategic locations for a sufficient period of time to permit the youth and adults of the area to visit them and participate in educational and cultural experiences otherwise unavailable to residents of these neighborhoods. It is anticipated that science workshops, seminars, lecture series, and symposiums to be staged in numerous community locations will foster diffusion of scientific knowledge throughout the county. To make this program possible, it is proposed that the community college and the institute of science pool their human and physical resources: institute personnel to prepare and maintain the exhibits and demonstrations, the community college to administer the program and provide the means for outreach. Joint appointment of scientific personnel and cooperative development of the programs are other features of the program.

Community Education

2. *The community college will place increased emphasis on community education for all age levels and all age groups.*

Increasingly, community education services of the community college are not limited to youth just out of high school or to adults of the community, but are provided for citizens of all age groups—including elementary and secondary school youngsters—with varying interests and points of view, and at all social and economic levels.

More and more these educational services are embracing the whole gamut of community life and are designed to prepare citizens to cope with rapid and sweeping social, political, and technological changes. Robert Havighurst has characterized these changes as "social processes" and has summarized them under five categories: (1) The expansion of human action in space and time; (2) mass production, automation, cybernation, and the changing significance of work; (3) metropolitanization; (4) world independence and cooperation; and (5) social integration (6).

Occupational demands today are such that the average worker in this country has more than a high school education and the average professional worker already has the equivalent of a master's degree. In order to remain contributory, a worker will have to prepare for several kinds of jobs during his life. For example, a young man beginning his work at age twenty can expect to make seven different job changes during his stay in the labor force. Experience indicates that at every age, 50 percent of the men in a job one year will be in a different job the succeeding year. And the continuing trend will be toward more and more semiprofessional occupations as the art and technology of automation develops.

But, in addition to meeting manpower training needs, the community college is concerned about the general education of all the citizens of its district community. Through its community services function, it is now possible for the first time in history for members of the community to have educational opportunity at their doorstep.

While education formerly concentrated its efforts primarily on changing the student in his relationship with himself (skills for self-improvement), it must now provide him with the information and skills that contribute to social improvement. The community college must seek out and educate all sorts of potential leaders—those in the upper, middle, and lower classes—and teach them to become ceaselessly involved in public affairs.

The community college's unique qualities have given it a most significant role to play in community decision-making. As the "people's college" it recognizes that an informed and responsible electorate is essential to a democratic nation if that nation is to survive and flourish; that "States are made . . . from the character of their citizens. . . ." The progress of the United States as a dynamic and free society is a result in part of the fact that it has provided more educational opportunities of more kinds for more people than any other nation.

The community education program will place increased emphasis on activities for the effective use of leisure time because of the trend toward a shorter work week, an earlier retirement age, and a longer life span. Commenting on increased leisure, Joan Littlewood has proposed to create in London a university of the street—an informal place where nothing is obligatory, anything goes. As a foretaste of the pleasures of 1984, her "Fun Palace" will feature (1) a fun arcade full of psychological and scientific games and tests with knowledge piped through juke-boxes; (2) musical programs for everyone including free instruction, and by night, jam sessions, jazz festivals, poetry, and dance; (3) a "science playground" supported by teaching films, closed-circuit television and working models; and (4) an acting area affording men and women from factories, shops, and offices the therapy of theater. At various points, sheltered or open, there will be screens on which closed circuit television will show, without editing or art, whatever is going on at a number of places in and out of London and in the complex itself (8:432–33).

Education for all age levels: Los Angeles Southwest College, California; State University of New York Agricultural and Technical College at Farmingdale; Miami-Dade Junior College, Florida; and Cuyahoga Community College, Ohio, offer examples of programs designed for groups not usually thought of as of "college age."

Eschewing to cater to any specific sex or age group, the new Los Angeles Southwest College, scheduled to open in September 1968, plans to place special emphasis on a unique program of community services for all of its publics. The magnitude of this undertaking is suggested by the fact that the socioeconomic range within the ten-mile area served by the college is from extreme poverty to moderate affluence. It is proposed that the entire campus of the college be open on Saturday from 8:30 a.m. until 2:00 p.m. to provide special science and mathematics explorations for youngsters from sixth through ninth grade; a parent-child exploration in economics and youth stock club, real or theoretical; a grooming clinic; a library reading circle for youngsters, fourth through seventh grades; individual program learning laboratory; a special reading class; Swedish gymnastics for all ages; music and art explorations for sixth through ninth graders; and vocational explorations for all levels. Ambitious as this program undoubtedly is, it cannot be denied that its successful implementation will go far toward meeting unspoken community needs.

A center for Community Educational Services has been established by the State University of New York Agricultural and Technical College at Farmingdale. Some 720 special programs were offered in 1967–68, accommodating 32,000 people. These programs included conferences, workshops, seminars, institutes, and other types of meetings, carefully tailored for persons from all age groups and all walks of life. Three programs, in which 247 persons participated, were federally funded under Title I of the Higher Education Act; namely, New Horizons for Later Years, Gericare-Aide Training, and Gateway to Careers for Women.

And Miami-Dade Junior College offered a noncredit short course for senior citizens explaining "their rights under the social security law" and enrolled fifty-four in English for the foreign-born. Another course, "Preparation Strings," attracted forty ranging from age four to adult. Also noncredit, the course was held on Saturday mornings.

In the summer of 1967, Baltimore Junior College developed a course especially geared to the needs of prospective college students who were planning to enroll at the college in September. The course was designed to answer the questions, how do I get started? what is college? how can I be a successful college student? Areas essential to success—a mature attitude, study skills, freshman writings, social adjustments—were discussed in detail. Interestingly, the dozen or so students who enrolled for the month-long short course were primarily from poverty areas.

Even more important than answering the questions posed by the Baltimore course, perhaps, is finding a satisfying response to: How do I make my life meaningful? Cuyahoga Community College is attempting to do just that for women through its project EVE, designed for widows, divorcees, and other women whose children are grown. Programs, offered both on campus and in the community, provide information, counseling, and referral services for the mature woman making decisions in the three EVE areas: (1) education to prepare the mature woman; (2) volunteer activities to which a significant contribution can be made; and (3) employment opportunities on a part-time or full-time basis. EVE offers individual counseling, group presentation of career information and employment opportunities, and group discussions of decisions facing the mature woman.

Training for business, industry, government, and professions: Most community colleges offer preservice and in-service noncredit short courses for employed adults as a major part of the community education program. Exemplars include Montgomery Junior College in Maryland; Suffolk County Community College in New York; Jamestown Community College, New York; Abraham Baldwin College in Georgia; Flint Community Junior College in Michigan; and Amarillo College, Texas.

In September 1966, Montgomery Junior College started the first non-credit evening program in the country for practicing dental assistants who wish to work toward certification. In a series of four courses, six preclinical offerings of the day program are combined. This series meets the requirements set down in 1960 by the American Dental Association and is kept comparable with the daytime program offerings. One course is offered each semester and only practicing assistants who have been employed as dental assistants for at least six months, are high school graduates, and have satisfactory typing ability are eligible to enroll. After completion of all four courses with satisfactory grades and approximately 700 hours of on-the-job, clinical experiences, an assistant is considered eligible for certification.

Suffolk County Community College has developed, in cooperation with the Civil Service Training Council, twenty-two in-service training courses offered at seven different locations throughout the county. County employees attend from 3:00 p.m. to 5:00 p.m. as part of their working day, their tuition being paid by the Council. Approximately fifty county executives participated in the six-week management training seminar for top executives, while the ten-week seminar for second-level executives attracted some 200. In most cases all expenses were paid by the county.

An in-service training program has been offered in a nearby electronics plant, the local telephone company, the tool company, and on-campus by Jamestown Community College in such diversified occupations as insurance, middle-management, engineering, and public school custodian and maintenance work. Ninety-eight engineers or engineering staff members participated in a five-week numerical control seminar offered on the college campus and 300 local business personnel attended an all-day seminar on collective bargaining.

On a level somewhat more professional than occupational, Jamestown Community College, in cooperation with the American Association of University Women, also developed an eight-week substitute teaching workshop. The purposes of the endeavor were to develop a pool of substitute teachers and to encourage others qualified to get into teaching. Sixty-four enrolled in the workshop, which was taught by local school principals. All costs for the workshop were borne by the AAUW.

Equally attractive have been two widely differing programs developed by Amarillo College, Texas. The first, a highly successful executive management seminar held in a downtown hotel and limited to twenty-five top executives on an invitational basis, has had quota enrollments each time it has been offered. And the second, an unusual approach to homemaking, drew approximately 600 women last year. Despite the fact that formal homemaking curriculums, both day and evening, have generally been quite unsuccessful in the community college, Amarillo's noncredit in-service training approach has proved the exception to the rule. Day and evening short courses in basic sewing, beginning sewing, tailoring, upholstering, and interior decoration are offered, and home visits are made by the instructor. The program appeals especially to young married women, who attend one day each week for two hours over a ten-week period.

Flint Community College also provides a program directed to meeting a specific need. This constitutes special preparation courses for chartered life insurance underwriters qualifying for licensing. These courses, each of which is related to a special examination, are offered in the afternoon one day a week for two and a half hours. Upon completion of the courses and passing satisfactorily the five examinations involved, students' licensing is confirmed.

But perhaps the most unusual in-service training program of all was found at Abraham Baldwin College where the offerings have been developed not for local community members but for missionaries working in sixteen different foreign countries. The program, titled "Agricultural Missions," in early 1967 brought twenty-five missionaries to the campus from a Friday noon to the following Monday morning for the discussion of such topics as "How Agricultural Research Can Help You Help People" and "Global Strategy Against Hunger." So successful was this session, that a follow-up program was held for a full week in May, 1967.

Human resource development: The community college is increasingly concerned about providing the reskilling and reendowment necessary for workers to remain productive; basic education for the functionally illiterate; "Head Start" type and occupational and basic skill programs for disadvantaged youth and adults; and special programs for the rapidly growing number of early retirees. Some outstanding activities in these areas were discovered during the course of this survey, and those in representative colleges are discussed here.

Cuyahoga Community College's unique project AIM, for example, is based on the premise that people should be trained for jobs that exist. Thus, in cooperation with the county welfare department, the college developed a program to train case worker aides and home health aides who could free well-paid professionals from many lower-level tasks and, at the same time, earn their own way in life. Forty women on welfare participated in the initial program five days a week, spending a half-day in class and a half-day on the job. Funded through the Cleveland Economic Opportunity office, the program allowed women enrolled in the noncredit courses to receive welfare checks as usual, plus 20 percent additional, and a transportation allowance. At the conclusion of their training, the women moved into jobs that paid more than the minimum for continuation on welfare. Such a program suggests one answer to the repeated complaint that the "hand-out" is not the solution to the economic problems of disadvantaged citizens.

Apparently subscribing to this point of view, New York City Community College offered two special manpower training programs aimed at helping deserving people to become self-sustaining. In the fall of 1966, fifteen disadvantaged young adults were placed in positions as college department aides as part of their full-time work experience. Trainees were also involved in group guidance sessions, individual counseling, and basic skills remediation. When the program terminated a year later, all participants had been placed in jobs related to the skills they had developed. A few entered New York City Community College as students, and one trainee joined the college staff as a full-time technical assistant. The other program, Key Punch Training, was developed at the request of the Two Bridges Neighborhood Council, a community action organization of Manhattan's lower east side, and the South Brooklyn Progress Center, an agency of the Human Resources Administration. The program's purpose was to provide short intensive training for 240 poverty area residents to equip them with requisite skills for immediate placement as key punch operators. A significant component of the program was the counseling, placement, and on-the-job follow-up of the students, all of which revealed the practical good sense of providing people with an opportunity to *be* and to *do*, constructively.

Similarly motivated programs have been worked out at other colleges as well. Baltimore (Maryland) Junior College, for one, has developed a new career program to educate persons, ages twenty-two and up, who have had job problems. Working under a $100,000 grant from the U.S. Department of Labor, personnel are trained at the job-entry level as psychology aides, home visitation aides, government service aides, data processing aides, and the like. This program, aimed at poverty and minority groups of whom some 300 are participating, requires students to spend a half-day in class and a half-day on the job, thus sustaining both interest and motivation.

Another program aimed at poverty and minority groups is Suffolk Community College's data processing (key punch) course, developed as an accelerated summer program. Enrolled were twenty people on county welfare who had been screened by the welfare department; and at the end of the six-week training period, all were placed in good jobs. So rewarding was this initial effort that the college is planning similar programs in basic drawing and machine operating.

Of course, other segments of the population besides the disadvantaged are of equal concern to the community college, not the least of which are those who can profit from technical-vocational education. Because of its demonstrated capabilities in this sphere of training, North Florida Junior College has been designated an area vocational school and, as such, houses on its campus a Vocational Center for high school students or others sixteen years and older. The Center, which was built at a cost of $400,000, is used extensively by the college for an adult vocational education program in the evening. And two Texas community colleges— Amarillo and Del Mar—are representative of community colleges that offer noncredit apprenticeship training. Approximately sixty students were enrolled at Amarillo in forty-eight-week courses in carpentry, painting, and electrical work; while at Del Mar, some 500 apprentices were in the program developed in cooperation with the local unions and industries. Instruction is offered for carpenters, electricians, ironworkers, instrumentation workers, painters, plumbers, sheet metal workers, and maintenance mechanics.

Some of these vocational fields are also covered by programs developed under the Manpower Development Training Act. During the last academic year at Westark Junior College, Arkansas, for example, 142 students were enrolled in MDTA day courses including dry cleaning, sheet metal fabrication, machine shop, stenography, auto mechanics, autobody, electricity, and drafting. And similar or supplemental MDTA offerings were available at San Antonio and St. Phillips colleges in Texas—to cite but two other examples. During the fall semester alone, eighty students were enrolled in medical secretary, legal secretary, and general secretary programs at San Antonio College; while St. Phillips College enrolled 160 students in welding, upholstery, rod and chainman, service station attendant, and legal secretary courses. Also at St. Phillips, sixty students were enrolled in the noncredit nurses' aide program, and 200 were taking the noncredit licensed vocational nurses training.

Big Bend Community College in Washington, concerned about women's welfare, is demonstrating that a community college can successfully handle training programs designed to upgrade and make employable women from among the disadvantaged and bypassed. The program, unique in the country for a community college, involves the provision on a contractual basis of several training programs for a Women's Job Corps Center. Two programs in the health occupations—licensed practical nurse and nurse's aide—are already being offered, and a third is in the process of development. This will be for hospital attendants with three options: laundryman, housekeeper, and food services aide, all of which provide meaningful and relatively remunerative occupations for women.

Meeting community needs: There are, of course, many community needs, which are identifiable in every community college district, and to which the college can respond. Cerritos College in California, Abraham Baldwin College in Georgia, Milwaukee Institute of Technology, North Florida Junior College, and Miami-Dade Junior College provide excellent examples of short courses offered in direct response to identified community needs.

Cooperating with fourteen community school districts, Cerritos College developed a forum on illegal drug traffic, titled "The Destroyers." The program, planned by the college's Civic Responsibility Committee, led to the revision of the curriculum in the fifth and sixth grades of the local school districts.

Abraham Baldwin College offered an all-day short course on tourism in cooperation with five local organizations. Purpose of the course was to assist south Georgia business firms in developing a more extensive tourist trade and to improve the services available to the tourists.

A three-session fire prevention and plant protection school was organized by Milwaukee Institute of Technology in cooperation with the Metropolitan Milwaukee Association of Commerce. The school is open to all interested employees of Milwaukee business, some 3,000 of whom participated in the three sessions during the last year.

North Florida Junior College offers a high school drama institute open to high school juniors and seniors during the summer each morning for six weeks. Acting, makeup, stage craft, scenery, and other aspects of dramatics are covered. The college has also been asked to develop a short course in simple electricity for local 4-H Clubs. The program for forty boys would be offered in the evening for ten weeks.

And Miami-Dade Junior College offered a six-session short course on the principles and techniques of exporting, titled "Export '67." The program was developed in cooperation with the United States Department of Commerce, the South Florida Regional Export Expansion Council, and the International Affairs Council of the Miami-Dade Chamber of Commerce. The college also organized a family camping clinic open to the entire family. The six-session clinic covered everything from "what's cooking" to "what to wear."

Diversification of Media

3. *The community college will utilize a greater diversification of media in meeting community needs and interests.*

No longer can it be said that the community college fulfills its community responsibility by merely offering a new course "any time ten or more citizens want it, if teacher, space, funds, and equipment are available." Increasingly, the class is only one of numerous media utilized in the program of community services: telecommunications; seminars and symposiums; performing groups; self-instructional packages, educational and cultural tours; workshops and conferences; counseling and consultative services; research and planning; recreational activities; science experiments and exhibitions; facility usage; leadership, coordination and advisory assistance; public lectures and fine arts events.

Short courses: Even short courses offered under the program of community services take on a different format, as illustrated by anecdotes from Bakersfield College in California and Flint Community Junior College in Michigan.

The Biostratigraphy Seminar sponsored by Bakersfield College is an example of the community appealing to the local community college to solve a problem for them. Since petroleum is one of the major industries of the Bakersfield area, a number of paleontology laboratories are maintained there. Paleontologists, feeling a need to keep current with developments in the field, asked the College to formulate the program. An advisory committee made up of representatives from the petroleum industry and the college was set up to discuss the problem and the seminar was begun in 1963. It consists of a series of eight lectures during the academic year presented by paleontologists, stratigraphers, and geologists from nearby universities, and leading scientists employed by the oil companies themselves. The topics deal with the latest research and findings pertinent to the work of the seminar attendees. Now in its sixth year, it continues to fill a need for the petroleum industry.

Less protracted but of equal value to the women for whom it was organized was the all-day conference in the local YWCA sponsored by Flint Community Junior College. Cosponsored by the Volunteer Bureau and the YWCA, the program featured afternoon workshops geared to answer the questions posed by community women concerning employment, volunteer service, and education opportunities in the areas of health occupations, sales and service, teaching, clerical and business, and creative arts. So that women with small children might not be excluded from attending the conference, nursery school service for youngsters two to five years old was provided for a minimal fee. Unspectacular though this kind of community service may be, there is no denying that it fills an urgent need in many areas of the country.

Telecommunications: An increasing number of community colleges employ educational telecommunications media in meeting the needs of residents of the college district. Representative examples are San Antonio College in Texas, the Foothill Junior College District in California, Milwaukee Institute of Technology, San Bernardino Valley College in California, Los Rios Junior College District in California, and Amarillo College in Texas.

San Antonio College operates radio station KSYM-FM Monday through Friday from 4:00 p.m. to 9:00 p.m. as an education station meeting the diversified interests of the San Antonio community and surrounding areas. The station also serves as a teaching aid for students enrolled in the broadcasting curriculum.

KFJC, the Foothill Junior College District's educational FM radio station, is used extensively in the district's community services program. Many cultural and public events held on the Foothill or De Anza College campus are taped for rebroadcast, in addition to programs especially prepared for the community. And the station beams In-School Programming, including science, fine arts, and literature, to public schools of the college district from 1:00 p.m. to 2:30 p.m. each Monday through Friday.

Milwaukee Institute of Technology's educational television stations, WMUS and WMUT, provide cultural and educational entertainment to the community; telecast lessons to selected classroom audiences; and offer technical and practical instruction to students enrolled in the telecasting department. A number of telecourses are offered during the week's schedule in addition to special programs in which WMUS cooperates with the Public Library, the Public Museum, and the Milwaukee area's music, art, and theater organizations.

Since 1962 San Bernardino Valley College has operated KVCR-TV as an educational television station functioning in four areas: (1) college-level instruction, using both open and closed circuit; (2) instruction and enrichment for approximately 100,000 elementary and secondary students in classrooms throughout San Bernardino County, including Spanish at grade levels kindergarten through high school and special in-service teacher training; (3) programs of general education, cultural, and public affairs for citizens at large in the college district; and (4) along with KVCR-TV's sister station KVCR-FM, broadcast training for students preparing for careers in professional radio and television. Earlier the college also utilized its television and FM radio stations in its unique Community Education Project, a special effort to involve greater numbers of people in the study and improvement of communities in the college district.

In order to provide equal educational opportunity throughout its 2,600 square mile district, Los Rios Junior College District is developing the concept of the Little Red Electronics Schoolhouse. These one-room facilities, stocked with thirty carrels equipped for audio-tutorial study with approximately 100 channels to the adjoining control room, would be constructed in five outlying pockets of population. Each of the one-room buildings would be staffed with a tutor-counselor and an electronic library aide. The District Educational Resource Center, staffed to develop audiovisual and curricular materials, program tapes, videotapes, and supplementary material, would serve the projected five colleges as well as the electronic schoolhouses. A mobile library and a mobile science laboratory would be stocked and follow a regular schedule of visits to each facility.

Amarillo College was instrumental in organizing a communications network designed to link junior colleges and four-year colleges within the region. The Western Information Network Association, recently authorized by the Texas legislature, is composed of five other junior colleges, six private four-year colleges, and six public four-year colleges and universities. The network will include two-way television and an information retrieval system. Members of the community, as well as college students, will benefit from programming which the network will make possible.

Tours and field trips: Four California community colleges—Foothill College, American River Junior College, Mount San Antonio College, College of San Mateo—and Orange County Community College in New York have developed imaginative tour programs.

Foothill College, during August of 1967, organized a week-long nature field trip into the beautiful and rugged Minarets area of the Sierra Nevada for thirty-six members of the college community. A field coordinator and two instructors—one each in biology and geology—accompanied the group, thus providing an opportunity for instructional emphasis on the biological and geological features of the region.

Also in the realm of nature study are the somewhat unusual tours for community youngsters sponsored by two other California junior colleges. American River Junior College conducts tours of wild life areas for elementary and high school students, while Mount San Antonio takes elementary children on tours of its agricultural facilities. During the year, approximately 6,000 pupils participated in Mt. Sac's farm tour program.

On a much broader scale are the tours for adults developed by College of San Mateo and New York's Orange County Community College. During July and August of 1966, the latter sponsored a five-week, eight-nation tour of Europe, whose director was a member of the college sociology department. And College of San Mateo has scheduled for 1968 three trips into Mexico and South America: Field Study in Pre-Columbian Civilization in Mexico City and Field Study in Mayan Civilization, centering on the Yucatan Peninsula and Guatemala, both planned for nine days during Easter vacation; and a People-to-People Exploration of Central and South America to be undertaken during twelve weeks from June to early September.

Community performing groups: Community chorus, orchestra, and theater programs are provided by a number of community colleges. Representative examples are to be found in the Foothill Junior College District in California, Suffolk County Community College in New York, Montgomery Junior College in Maryland, and New York City Community College.

Somewhat paralleling the program at Del Mar College, Texas, reported in Chapter II, is that of Foothill Junior College District's Music Makers, which also encompasses three community performing groups. In the three years of its existence, the 140-voice symphonic choir, Schola Cantorum, has established itself as a major musical organization in the San Francisco Bay area, having performed in concert with both the San Francisco and the Monterey Peninsula symphony orchestras. Included in its four district concerts each year are both standard repertory and interesting new choral works. Equally popular is the Master Symphonia, formed in 1965 for community musicians whose abilities were of professional quality and whose preference was for a small, select chamber ensemble. Beginning with a nucleus of sixteen strings, it now is augmented by winds and brass to fit the instrumentation of its repertoire. For persons with similar abilities but who enjoy participating in a larger group, the Nova Vista Orchestra provides an aesthetic outlet, and represents the combined efforts of the community and the district's two colleges.

Similar musical activities sponsored as community services have been organized by Montgomery Junior College and New York City Community College. Although college students may participate in both groups, the Montgomery Symphony Orchestra and the Montgomery Light Opera Association are primarily for members of the community who are qualified in instrumental music, singing, and drama. The eighty-member orchestra is directed by a skilled conductor employed by the district, and plays a regular series of concerts in various parts of the county. And New York City Community College's Opera Workshop, although catering to a more restricted geographical area, nevertheless presents opera performances free to the local community besides providing valuable experience to the workshop's participating singers, stage directors, and pianists.

Concentrating rather more on theatrical productions than orchestral or operatic works is the college-community theater group organized by Suffolk County Community College. This group, composed of college students and members of the community, presents three plays and a musical each year, and it is not unusual for a play to run ten nights.

Consulting services: A number of colleges provide community consulting services; but a report on three New York community colleges that are typical—New York Community College, State University of New York Agricultural and Technical College in Farmingdale, and Suffolk County Community College—will suffice to indicate directions in which this trend may lead.

Under the Technical Service Act, a program of technical assistance to industry is being developed by New York City Community College in the areas of optics, data processing, and numerical control. The service will be in the form of technical bulletins, newsletters, and consultation. And State University of New York Agricultural and Technical College at Farmingdale already provides a wide array of consulting services to the community; e.g., a farmer may bring in a piece of sod for analysis, or staff members may be called upon to consult in landscaping. In one instance, two members of the horticulture faculty participated in a study of a blighted urban area, surveying it and making recommendations at no charge to the community. As a result of these services, the community appropriated $46,000 to clean up and landscape the area. Suffolk County Community College has also provided consulting services for a water company and economic consulting services for community agencies.

Community counseling: Even more widespread than consulting services are the testing and counseling and guidance services provided by many community colleges to district residents of all ages who are not enrolled in formal classes. Examples of these services, among others, can be seen at Westark Junior College in Arkansas, Suffolk County Community College in New York, and Flint Community Junior College in Michigan.

Typical of the testing services for business and industry which Westark Junior College has provided are those administered by college personnel, over a period of four to six months, to candidates for top executive positions in Gerber Food Products Company. The efficient screening made possible by these tests prompted other local firms—in particular, insurance companies and pharmaceutical houses—to request similar services for their supervisory personnel. And selected supervisors and middle-management personnel from another local firm were given tests to find potential promotionable material prior to attending a ten-week in-plant training program covering organization and management, cost accounting and control, methods of analysis, and English and report writing.

Quite different in nature but performing a valuable service to the community is Suffolk County Community College's Project SEARCH, a community counseling program geared to the needs of underprivileged but capable high school dropouts. Participants were identified by community groups such as high schools and the welfare department, personally contacted, and invited to attend a series of ten meetings held in their area. Through group discussions, individual counseling, audiovisual materials, and testing, the individuals in the program explored their abilities, deficiencies, goals, relationship to society, and the vocational and educational opportunities available if they had college experience. Of the 128 who took advantage of the program, eleven were accepted into full-time study at the college, and a large number enrolled as part-time students; twenty-five were provided a neighborhood aid course and are working for the Office of Educational Opportunity; twelve were given a clerk-typist course, seven of whom passed Civil Service exams and are now employed by the county. The growing need for the development of a licensed practical nursing program was also identified through the counseling process, and plans for its initiation are being considered.

Although a good deal has been said about programs for mature women, Flint Community Junior College's Community Counseling for Mature Women, established under a grant from Title I of the Higher Education Act, probably is unique. Two trained counselors work out of a center on campus and pay particular attention to the needs of lower economic and inner city groups. Evening and Saturday appointments are made as well as during the business day. Goals of the program are to provide educational counseling, vocational information, testing, and follow-up where needed; and to refer women to community agencies when appropriate. Communication, liaison, and cooperative channels have been established with such groups as social agencies; professional, service, fraternal organizations; adult high schools; area colleges; public agencies; Parent-Teacher Associations and other school groups; and the Mott Vocational Education and Retraining Department. Certainly, with all of these avenues open to them, the mature women of Flint, through the community services program of their community college, have been provided with the opportunity to take their useful and rewarding place in a society of which they form a most important part.

Science services: Representative of community colleges maintaining planetariums is San Antonio College in Texas. The planetarium serves an average of 40,000 youths and adults from the community each year. Lecture-demonstrations are held in the planetarium daily; every elementary school in the city has participated in the program.

Recreation: El Camino College in California uses two pools for ten weeks each summer to teach approximately 2,500 community youngsters to swim or swim better. The two-week training program is run in two shifts each day, 8:00 a.m. to 3:00 p.m. and 3:00 p.m. to 10:00 p.m. The success of the program is attested to each year when swimming tickets go on sale; people bring sleeping bags and begin forming long lines at 4:00 a.m.

Cultural programs: Santa Monica City College's children's theater, Modesto Junior College's festival and tour, and Pasadena City College's Tuesday evening series are excellent examples of cultural programs provided by California community colleges.

Attracting national attention, Santa Monica City College's Theatre for Children was conceived in 1952 by the head of the theatre arts department. The annual program of theatre productions, developed in cooperation with the Parent-Teachers' Association and the elementary school principals, was designed specifically for children in elementary school and is presented in the spring. More than 6,000 children are admitted annually to some twenty different shows, which are performed on Friday and Saturday afternoons. Some must be turned away from this popular program where a "Mistress of the Revels" greets the children before the play and invites them to the autograph party that follows each performance. Many of the plays are specifically written for college actors to perform for children. An "Oscar" was awarded to this unusual theater project by the *Journal of Elementary Education*.

Modesto Junior College sponsors an annual Bret Harte Festival and Mother Lode Tour in April for students and members of the community. The week-long festival includes such on-campus events as symposiums, movies, plays, and student competition. The Mother Lode Tour follows on Saturday and is designed to visit the sites mentioned in Bret Harte's short stories. Tour activities include lectures and dramatizations from literature using the Mother Lode country as the setting.

And now in its forty-first year, Pasadena City College's Tuesday Evening Forum brings such noted persons as Dr. Ralph Bunche, Ray Bradbury, Dr. S. I. Hayakawa, and David Schoenbrun to the campus weekly from October through April.

Community Development

4. *The community college will increasingly utilize its catalytic capabilities to assist its community in the solution of basic educational, economic, political, and social problems.*

In the process of becoming an educational resource center, the community college is dynamically relating its programs to the existing and emerging needs of its district community. Through action programs aimed at closing the nullah now dividing the inner city from the outer community; baseline data from community studies; the leadership and advisory assistance of college personnel in the mobilization of community resources;

long-range planning; workshops, institutes and conferences; and the organization of community coordinating councils and other needed groups, the community college is becoming an agency for social change.

But for the community development program to achieve its maximum potential, the mobilization of the total resources of the community is required. The natural role of the community college in the program is that of a catalytic force—an agency for social change. Citizens in a democratic society must learn to work together to analyze common needs and to achieve desired goals.

The time has come, according to Samuel B. Gould, for this country to recognize that it is facing ". . . problems of illiteracy, of untrained citizens incapable of maintaining economic independence in our technological world, of poverty and disease and the resultant disorders these are presently spawning in all our cities, of the steady deterioration of that priceless asset of democracy—the dignity of the individual." He has concluded that the leaders of educational institutions must take the initiative in an attack upon urban problems. They must not "climb back into the tower and pull the ladder up" (3).

Harold Gores, president of the Educational Facilities Laboratories, Inc., has agreed with Gould: "Education, and particularly the community college, may be the best hope of the inner city. . . . Maybe it [the community college] has to be put into the neighborhood business. The people trust it. They depend upon it" (12).

Programs for disadvantaged: A number of community colleges in urban areas are developing both attractive and rewarding educational programs for the disadvantaged. Examples included in this report are found at Westark Junior College in Arkansas, Cabrillo College and San Jose City College in California, New York City Community College, Baltimore Junior College in Maryland, Hudson Valley Community College in New York, and the Peralta Colleges of California.

During the past year, 192 disadvantaged students have participated in the Neighborhood Youth Corps program at Westark Junior College. Students spend approximately half of their time in remedial writing, reading, and arithmetic and the other half in automobile mechanics, body, and welding programs working in groups of ten; a beginning and advanced stenography program for girls is offered during the day. The students, high school dropouts in their upper teens, spend approximately eight hours a week in the program, and the rest of the time in paid jobs that have been arranged by the Youth Corps.

Another Neighborhood Youth Corps project is the educational aide training program which New York City Community College has developed for approximately 1,000 trainees. Funded by a $750,000 grant from the Human Resources Administration, the one-year training program is designed to prepare these young people for the high school equivalency examination and arm them with necessary skills. At the conclusion of their training period, they will be employed by the New York City Board of Education.

Assured employment provides strong motivation for participants to remain in both the Westark and New York City programs; yet the prospect—not merely the promise—of an improved way of life offered by several community colleges has likewise stimulated many disadvantaged persons to put forth maximum effort. Baltimore Junior College, for example, has initiated two programs for youngsters from culturally disadvantaged sections of Baltimore. Some eighty tenth- and eleventh-grade students from Baltimore High School are participating in the Upward Bound Program, whose purpose is to increase the motivation of culturally deprived but promising students to remain in school, achieve better, and seek college goals. The other program, Operation: College Horizons, is geared to the needs of junior and senior high school students and their parents. The purposes of this project, which began in 1963, are (a) to provide an understanding of the educational, vocational, social, and financial benefits to be derived from college attendance; (b) to provide facts relating to curricular offerings of the junior college; (c) to provide facts concerning college costs and available financial aids; and (d) to provide an understanding of how progress in junior and senior high school, including skills and study habits, is related to progress in college.

And the Peralta Colleges are developing an extensive program for the culturally disadvantaged of the inner city. A major aim is to develop the kind of community pride and resourcefulness required to change the nature and quality of life for those who remain in the inner city. Features of the program include (a) a student service corps to carry on a work-study service program of community outreach development in the inner city; (b) community development centers to provide educational and counseling services in the inner city, serving as focal points for workshops; (c) an enrichment program of workshops in art, music, and drama, to be supplemented by recreational, social, cultural, and educational experiences at the block, neighborhood, and community levels; and (d) a scholarship subsistence program.

Perhaps one of the more difficult tasks the community college has to perform in connection with such programs is stimulating interest in them among the people they are designed to serve. This cannot be left until the hopes and enthusiasms usually characteristic of childhood in almost any environment have been drained away. Perhaps with this in mind, Cabrillo College and San Jose City College in California have developed tutoring programs for children of minority groups in their districts. At Cabrillo, students volunteer their services as tutors, while participating students at

San Jose receive a small stipend for their activities. Cabrillo's program for Mexican-American children, titled "Follow-Up" and begun as an adjunct to project "Head Start," was cosponsored by the Santa Cruz County Human Rights Action Committee and operated at three centers: one at the YWCA, one at a local church, and the other at the civic auditorium. Twenty-seven college students and thirteen adults worked in the three centers, where some sixty children participated in the six-week summer program. Supplies were donated by local merchants, and city councilmen hosted the student tutors at a wind-up dinner. The San Jose City College program was extended to include Negro as well as Mexican-American children, and the college is also developing special recreation activities for members of these minority communities within the college district.

Hudson Valley Community College operates the State University Urban Center in the Capital District in three locations, but has one over-all purpose: to provide educational opportunities, counseling, and occupational skills training for those members of the local community who are unemployed, underemployed, and educationally disadvantaged. A vocational program is backed up by one strongly academic in nature, in the hope of raising the quality of life of the students and of the community as a whole.

Community leadership: Although awareness of opportunities for lifting themselves from their depressed state is important for ghetto residents, they need also to be shown how to take advantage of such opportunities. For this they require community leadership and advisory assistance both during their emergence into a more rewarding way of life and after gaining their first objectives. Excellent examples of service in these areas are provided by Foothill College and the Peralta Colleges as well as New York City Community College.

Carrying these information dissemination services somewhat further and providing direct instruction in a specific field of endeavor, the Peralta Colleges are developing an unusual training program for the occupants of an apartment house in the inner city. The training program, to be conducted from a year to two years in the 140 unit apartment house in East Oakland, will include a series of short courses on budgeting, management, planning, and recreation for the purpose of preparing the residents to take over the management of the house as a cooperative.

Also encouraging to the development of initiative among the disadvantaged is the program of advisory assistance to emerging small businesses in the South Brooklyn poverty area of Greater New York being planned by New York City Community College.

Community action: Helping inner-city residents to enjoy a fuller life is, of course, but one aspect of the community college's commitment to its community services function, and constitutes a single segment of the college's contribution to total community development. Excellent examples of short courses in this area are found in numerous college districts throughout the country, some of the more salient of which are the following.

Rockland Community College, New York, in cooperation with thirty-two social agencies, developed a ten-session short course, "Introduction to Community Service," whose purposes were to recruit volunteers for community service and to present the value of social work. Totally funded by a grant from the State Department of Mental Hygiene, the short course was free of charge to the twenty-two enrolled.

Two short courses in the community development area were organized by Jamestown Community College. Developing and managing rural land for country living attracted 140 persons from the community. The four-week course was cosponsored by the Cooperative Extension Association of Chautauqua County Agricultural Division, and was designed to help prospective and rural land owners in the aspects of buying, developing, and managing rural lands and the related natural resources. The second seminar, also offered in four parts, was cosponsored by Fedonia State College and was concerned with the problems of Lake Chautauqua pollution.

Cerritos College, in cooperation with its research and development committee, sponsored a special program in city beautification. The conference constituted an effort to coordinate the combined resources of civic, business, industrial, and education leaders to promote and develop courses of action for the improvement and continued development of the physical environment. Well attended kick-off breakfasts were held in five communities of the college district, followed by a workshop on city beautification held on the college campus. Fifty-four persons from the total college district attended the workshop.

At the request of the Miami-Dade United Fund, Miami-Dade Junior College has developed a special training program for personnel of agencies supported by the United Fund. The short course concentrates on accounting standards applicable to United Fund budgeting and the preparation of budget forms.

Westark Junior College, in Arkansas, in response to threatened cessation of intercity bus service in the Fort Smith area, sponsored three seminars of three sessions each concerned with transit system problems. The goal of the seminars was to provide an educational opportunity for local citizens, municipal officials, and community planners to become aware of the basic practices and problems in the operation of a city transit system. Extensive use was made of data from the "Fort Smith Urban Transit Study" conducted for the University of Arkansas, Arkansas State Highway Department, and the Fort Smith-Sebastian County Planning Commission by a private consulting firm.

Miami-Dade Junior College has also developed a pilot program for the training and counseling of selected staff members of the economic opportunity program. The pilot program will include two sections of approximately ten persons each, the experience gained to be used in modifying the program for presentation to subsequent sections. It has been found that the neighborhood worker seems to lack skills in meeting, interviewing, and persuading people, and, after taking on the job, feels and acts as if he no longer belongs to the neighborhood. Groups of ten each, randomly selected from the neighborhood workers, will meet one night each week for two and a half hours for ten weeks. Two trained clinical psychologists will serve as facilitators for the sessions, helping workers to discover solutions to their problems.

Community research and planning: The community college's role in community research is exemplified by Bakersfield College in California.

The Bakersfield College Research Bureau, under the direction of a college staff member, was established about four years ago to perform a coordinating function and to provide research service to community organizations. Members of the college faculty, through the Bureau, conducted numerous studies and an analysis of business data for the county was published monthly in a local chamber of commerce publication. In the last year, the Research Bureau, having fulfilled immediate needs, has been less active.

Organization of community groups: New York City Community College has proposed the establishment of an Economic Opportunity Training Institute at the South Brooklyn Community Progress Center. The training program would be designed by a task force in response to problems and deficiencies that have been pointed out by the Center's clientele as well as its professional staff. During phase I, the primary objective of the task force would be not to provide training but to design it. Specific training, based upon needs identified in phase I, would be offered during phase II. The general need for training programs at such centers is evident in almost daily reports of abortive community action programs that fail because of conflict and/or misunderstanding between professional and nonprofessional staff or between staff and community.

Cultural Development

5. *The community college will be increasingly concerned about the cultural growth of its community and state.*

That this trend is already taking shape has been evident in many communities for some time. A survey of developments in California four years ago, for example, resulted in this conclusion: "California communities from the Sierra to the sea and the Siskiyous to the Mexican border are experiencing a cultural, social, and intellectual renaissance. And much of the credit for the community rebirth is due to California's seventy-one [now eighty] public junior colleges and their programs of community services" (4:14).

Although one might think that cultural renaissance is too grand a term to apply here, actually it is rather precise. For a description of the Renaissance Age is a description of today—one of expanding interest in the arts, creativity in science, and concern for humanity.

There is no reason to believe that these expanding areas will shortly reach their outer boundaries; indeed, to the contrary, as ideas are explored and values rethought, as knowledge is improved and the importance of things already known is placed in proper perspective through boldly structured community services programs, outer boundaries will disappear and with them will go the fragmentation now characterizing so much of American life.

Cultural centers: Flint Community Junior College and Macomb County Community College in Michigan, Del Mar College in Texas, Cerritos College in California, Bucks County Community College in Pennsylvania, Pasadena City College in California, and Rockland Community College in New York see their roles as cultural centers.

Flint Community Junior College is developing, in a wooded area adjoining the college campus, a cultural center that includes an intimate theater, an art center, auditorium, planetarium, museum, and a public library. The DeWaters Art Center is composed of a main art gallery, twelve art classrooms and studios, and two glassed-in courtyards. It is the home of the Flint Institute of the Arts. The Robert T. Longway Planetarium is one of only ten major planetariums in the United States. The circular chamber at the center of the dome seats 292 people. A telescope observation platform is in an adjoining annex. The F. A. Bower Theatre, a fully equipped facility with seating capacity of 352, is used for presentations of the Flint Community Players and for college theatrical productions. The Sloan Panorama of Transportation Museum presents displays that portray the growth of Flint as a major automotive manufacturing center. Yet to be completed is the James H. Whiting Auditorium, which will accommodate an audience of approximately 2,100.

And Macomb County Community College has proposed a college-community center to be constructed on its campus. The center would serve as the location for diversified activities for a wide variety of individuals and groups. These activities would be educational, cultural, and social. Participants would be college students, service groups, professional groups, faculty and nonaffiliated off-campus groups.

Through its extensive cultural program, Del Mar College has become a cultural center for the entire college district. For example, the college has organized four performing groups—a chamber orchestra, a chorale, choral ensemble, and a full symphony orchestra. Private or class music instruction is provided for adults and children. The auditorium and other college facilities are used extensively by local cultural organizations. Festivals and series presentations include the summer band concert on the Corpus Christi waterfront; art exhibition series, including a national sculpture and small drawing competition; faculty concert series; festival of contemporary music; the Buccaneer Music Festival; and the Collegium Musicum series of lectures and concerts.

Cerritos College has established a highly successful Music Conservatory program offering small class instruction to music students within the district from ages nine to twenty-one. In 1966–67, 800 students participated on weekends and in the later afternoons on the Cerritos campus as well as in the various communities within the district. The program was correlated very carefully with the existing district music education programs of local schools. Thus, a new dimension was added to the existing programs, raising the quality of individual student performance and the quantity of participation.

Perhaps the most ambitious and extensive composite of performing arts activities undertaken by a two-year college to date was initiated in the spring of 1967 by Bucks County Community College. A multifaceted program based upon experimental theater, children's theater, elementary and secondary school visitations, an art festival, and a college-sponsored professional repertory company provided the laboratory or apprenticeship experiences for the artists in training. The various facets of the program utilized the students and faculty of the college, the many talented amateurs and the excellent little theater groups performing in Bucks County, semiprofessionals, and guest professionals. Specifics of the program are Eight O'Clock Theater, including dramatic readings, original plays, student-directed one-act plays, recitals and contemporary theater, and a children's theater tour. A resident repertory theater company of approximately twenty nonunion community professionals performs for the Bucks County public a season of six classic plays from October through April at the Bucks County Playhouse. As an adjunct to the repertory theatre, the college will provide the services of a teacher and actor assistants to visit each of the county's participating elementary and secondary schools four times during the course of the theater season. Visits encompass discussion of plays, the play which is to be performed next, its background as a preview to attending the performance, a follow-up review of the performance, and dramatic readings and recitations by repertory players. Costs were initially borne by the Bucks County Arts Foundation.

Pasadena City College in California cosponsors an annual four-day conference, Writers' Week, with the writers' clubs and classes of the area.

Beginning in 1955 as the result of a request from the Pasadena Writers' Club, it takes the form of a lecture series with a unifying theme. Moderated by a local author and adult education teacher, four "theme" lectures are presented, one each morning, and guest lecturers are introduced who lecture in their special subject fields. Question and answer periods are provided; no registration fee is charged. In planning the conference, writers' clubs' representatives bring lists of writers or editors they would especially like to hear and fields of writing in which they are most interested. Contacts with some excellent writers for guest lecturers have been made through these representatives. About 200 persons are in attendance at each session. In accordance with state regulations governing lecture series, registration and attendance records are kept. The feature of the conference that receives most favorable comment is the unifying theme, supported by the opening lecture each day. The moderator defines the theme the first morning, discussing one facet of it. Each morning another facet is added and preceding lectures are tied into it. Because of this the audience leaves the conference with a central idea expanded and supported by different writers each in his own special way.

Rockland Community College has taken a number of steps toward the creation of a cultural center in the community. Conversations have been held with representatives of community organizations regarding the building on campus of a museum in cooperation with the Rockland County Historical Society; a theatre and/or auditorium that might be designed to serve the suburban symphony, choral society, and the local opera group as well as college performing groups, road companies, and other professional appearances; and a planetarium. In 1964, the community college offered a week's program of events designed to illustrate and discuss the idea of a cultural center. A number of sessions were directly concerned with planning improved cultural facilities. One of the outcomes of these discussions, attended by thirty-one official representatives from seventeen Rockland county cultural organizations, was the creation of a county arts council.

Arts councils: Delta College in Michigan and Monterey Peninsula College in California were instrumental in the formation of community arts councils.

Delta College organized and sustains the Saginaw Valley Arts Council, which is housed on the college campus. Some forty organizations from the three counties comprising the college district are members of the Council. The Council publishes an annual calendar; functions as a clearinghouse for the scheduling of events; operates a central arts information office at the college, which answers questions pertaining to the arts, whether local or international; and is undertaking a new program over the college-owned educational television station in which the area arts activity will be highlighted.

The Arts Coordinating Council of the Monterey Peninsula was spearheaded by Monterey Peninsula College. Twenty-five members from Peninsula communities belong to the Council, which has as its long-range purpose the planning of improved facilities for all the arts, leading to a coordinated center. The Council presently serves as a clearinghouse for dates of special events, publishes a regular calendar of the arts activities, and is developing a talent file of area artists, musicians, and performers. It also serves as the united voice in the community affairs of the arts.

Master planning: About two years ago, the Community Services Committee of the California Junior College Association proposed to influential state legislators that a master plan for the cultural and recreational development of the state of California be developed. In so doing, it was pointed out that sixty-five junior college districts (large political subdivisions that blanket the length and breadth of the state) provide a unique and logical network for the cultural development of the state. A trilateral approach to the cultural and recreational development through the junior college districts, the local citizenry, and the state's Arts Commission, according to the proponents, would ensure for California a state cultural and recreational program second to none. However, there was no immediate response.

College-Community Interaction

6. *The community college will place greater emphasis on interaction with its community.*

Increasingly, it is being recognized that the effective program of community services is built upon (1) a solid foundation of citizen participation and college-community interactions and (2) a thorough understanding of the community. Citizens actually participate in the planning, maintenance, and evaluation of the program; and the college, recognizing that it must be *of* the community and not just *in* it, participates in community life. In such a way mutual interaction is achieved. As a corollary, the importance of understanding the community cannot be overemphasized, and the administrator is effective only when he "is aware of the need for comprehensive and almost encyclopedic knowledge of his community" (2:12). Such knowledge is essential if the community services program is to be tailored to meet community needs, and if the college is to become the locus for community development (11:5).

The community is also a most valuable living laboratory for the enrichment of the total college curriculum. Activities might include field trips to art galleries, businesses and industries, city and county governmental agencies, and the like; utilization of the community for studies, surveys, and polls; joint programs with business and government such as business-education day, career programs, students in government; utilization of special community facilities and equipment such as hospitals; the participation of community leaders in the school program as speakers and resource persons for classes and school organizations, and as advisers in the development of curriculums and special programs.

Institutional synergy: This term has been defined as the simultaneous action of separate agencies, which together have a greater total effect than the sum of their individual efforts. Excellent examples of this phenomenon can be seen at Essex Community College in Maryland; Rockland Community College, Jamestown Community College, and State University of New York Agricultural and Technical College at Farmingdale; Oakland Community College in Michigan; and Rock Valley Community College in Illinois.

Illustrative of this term is the Health and Education Campus being developed by Essex Community College, Franklin Square Hospital, and the Baltimore County Health Department. Located on a 220-acre campus, the three agencies (soon to include a day care center for the mentally retarded, a rehabilitation nursing home, and possibly others) working together, sparking ideas with experiments, meeting local and regional needs as well as mutual needs, offer unusual opportunities in fulfilling the educational and health needs of the community. Examples of cooperation include the sharing of physical facilities in human resources, the joint development of paramedical curriculums, identifying new areas for which training is needed but not presently available, and continuing education programs for patients and community and through closed-circuit television.

Amarillo College is currently developing, in cooperation with local health agencies, a School of Health Occupations to be housed on the new Amarillo Medical Center Campus now under construction. The 396-acre campus will house approximately fifty-three million dollars in medical facilities, including seven hospitals. The Center has been planned to serve a four-state area. Amarillo College's School of Health Occupations will place particular emphasis on special health care training needs.

Since 1965, Rockland Community College has been involved in the area of community health and health education made possible by the support of the Edna McConnell Clark Foundation. The project includes the development of a Community Health Council, an agency concerned with the coordination of community health services and community planning for meeting health manpower needs, an in-service Health Education Center offering refresher and upgrading courses, clinics, and workshops for all health professionals and workers in need of and interested in education.

Hudson Valley Community College has played a leading role in setting up a community health planning agency and has gained the cooperation of two other colleges, three local hospitals, the county medical society, the county health society, a research institute, a number of leading industries, and individuals active in government, professional services, and unions in this endeavor. A community health profile is being made to help pinpoint health needs of the area. It is hoped that duplications of service can be avoided and that, by pooling their resources, the area hospitals can provide needed facilities that the individual hospitals could not afford. Office space, personnel, and data processing facilities on the college campus will be used to implement the expansion of the present study.

Subscribing to the thesis that the needs of the college and the needs of the community are compatible, Rockland Community College is developing its college library as a strong community-serving central reference and research library to complement existing library services in the county. The eight public school superintendents of the county are also interested in cooperating with the college toward creating a media center capable of sending educational programs to all of the schools of the county, as well as housing programmed instruction and other forms of instructional technology.

At Jamestown Community College, the entire campus has become an art gallery. Approximately 100 paintings of Chautauqua County artists are constantly on display in hallways and offices throughout the campus on a twelve-month basis, under the sponsorship of the 125-member Chautauqua County Society of Artists, with paintings being changed once a month. In fact, so successful has Jamestown's total community services program proved to date, that the college is now planning to establish a Community Service Center in the heart of Jamestown. Plans are to house the community service program and counseling services on the main floor, drawing municipal and social agencies now spread throughout the community to share this excellent downtown facility. In this manner it is hoped that a comprehensive community service program will be provided to those who most need the joint services of all these agencies and who currently are least aware or able to avail themselves of the services.

Examples of institutional synergy on a more restricted scale are nonetheless impressive by their accomplishment. The State University of New York Agricultural and Technical College at Farmingdale, for instance, has made available college facilities to the Amityville Play School. This nonprofit, cooperative nursery school operated for a number of years out of a local church, but is now located in a renovated building on the campus. Some thirty children are enrolled in the play school, which also serves as an observation laboratory for college students enrolled in the two-year Nursery Education Training Program.

Oakland Community College provides space for the Recordings for the Blind, a national nonprofit organization, which produces free recorded textbooks and other educational material for blind students and adults. Recordings for the Blind is a voluntary organization designed to enable the blind to secure the education essential to their becoming independent, productive members of society.

And at Rock Valley College, thirty-three companies cooperate in its unique Career Advancement Program. Each of these companies hires two employees, one to work in the mornings and one in the afternoons, and both to spend the other half-day at the college. The original request for 159 trainees has now grown to 174. Participating companies pay a $25 enrollment fee plus $5.00 for each trainee they request; send company personnel to visit high schools and give the students the company point of view; place advertisements in local newspapers and on radio and television; pay costs for brochures, mailing pieces, and other publicity. For the most part, students apply directly to the companies in which they are interested and at each company they must go through the regular employment processes of interviewing and testing.

Advisory committees: Cerritos College in California is aided in the planning and implementation of its program of community services by a Citizens' Advisory Council and nine advisory committees. The Advisory Council, which meets approximately twice each year, is composed of the chairmen and vice-chairmen of all of the advisory committees. The committees include adult education, business, civic responsibility, community research and development, community volunteer services, fine arts, professions, recreation, and youth. The committees also sponsor a number of programs throughout the year.

Community surveys: As an aid to planning for the needs and desires of the adult population through its community services program, Central Florida Junior College conducted a survey by interviewing a rather large cross section of the college community. In addition to information on adult and vocational education, comments on the college as a whole were welcomed and some information may prove valuable in future site acquisition and planning for growth.

Community councils: Jamestown Community College in New York and Vincennes University Junior College in Indiana have organized effective community coordinating councils.

Jamestown Community College provided the moving force in organizing a Council of Social Agencies for local organizations. Prior to the organization of this Council, few persons knew of the social agencies or whom they were serving. As an outgrowth of the initial meeting called by representatives of the college, the executive directors of seventeen agencies now have established communication to the point where they are no longer competing but are cooperating with each other. Expanding from the thirteen agencies involved originally three years ago, a broader organization now called United Fund and Council of Southern Chautauqua County retains the college president as a representative although the college no longer provides the sustaining force. Students from Jamestown and the State University at Buffalo, as a side aspect of the program, now work in some of the community social agencies selected by the college.

Vincennes University Junior College has organized a council of top managers of industries in the area, which plans educational programs for the welfare of industry. And a management association of more than 200 members in this community of 20,000 meets every month for an educational meeting.

Community-college sponsorship: Joining forces with a community organization, North Florida Junior College has created the North Florida Junior College-Madison Artists Series Association. The Association sponsors a high level Artists Series Program for the college and community. Its board is composed of a president from the community, a vice-president from the college, three faculty members, three citizens, and three students. The board of directors of the Association makes the final selection on recommendations from the program committee, which is chaired by the board vice-president. College students are admitted free upon presentation of student activity cards. Other attendance is on the basis of a membership fee.

Cooperation With Other Agencies

7. *The community college will increasingly recognize the need for cooperation with other community and regional agencies.*

In order to avoid unnecessary duplication of services, a greater effort is being made by community college personnel to coordinate the community college program of community services with programs of other community and regional agencies, i.e., public schools, recreation districts, governmental agencies, museums, art galleries, libraries, and four-year colleges and universities.

Cooperation with other community colleges: Recognition of the need for cooperative programs in community services between neighboring community colleges is gaining ground. Examples are College of San Mateo and the Foothill Junior College District in California, three New York City community colleges, and seventeen Los Angeles area colleges.

The San Mateo and Foothill Junior College Districts in California have entered into a special training program, cosponsored by the Junior League of Palo Alto, for the purpose of training unpaid volunteers for the public schools. Funded by a $4,000 grant from the Junior League for a two-year period, the program consists of a series of seminars and workshops designed to train the volunteers in the various skills needed. Coordination and aid are being worked out with the Public Education Association's National School Volunteer Program and the Volunteer Bureau.

New York City Community College, the Borough of Manhattan Community College, and Bronx Community College in New York are cooperating in a program to train 300 welfare clients, aged twenty-two and above. At the conclusion of the eleven-month program, the participants will be employed as aides by the Board of Education, the Department for Social Services, and the Department of Hospitals. The program consists of fifteen hours a week of high school equivalency preparation and skills training and is funded under a $1,000,000 grant from the Human Resources Administration. Participants would spend half a day in-plant and half a day in classes.

Seventeen junior colleges of Los Angeles County are cooperating in the offering of a two-unit health education course over a local commercial television channel on Saturday mornings beginning with the spring semester 1968. All students in California may register for credit in the course.

An excellent example of statewide cooperation is found in the College Association for Public Events and Services in California. Thirteen junior colleges of the Greater San Francisco Bay area formed the College Association for Public Events and Services in 1963 for the purposes of block booking lectures and artists and exchanging packaged programs and experiences. During the first year four major speakers were block booked, saving colleges an estimated $20,000. For example, Erich Fromm spoke to nearly 30,000 persons from CAPES communities; he drew audiences of 2,500 in communities where several hundred had been the usual audience. Now in its fifth year, CAPES has incorporated and expanded to seventy-seven members, including some four-year colleges. CAPES employs a full-time executive secretary and has offices in San Francisco.

Following suit, Oakland Community College in Michigan was instrumental in organizing the College Association for Public Events and Services—Michigan. Seventeen community colleges and nine four-year colleges have joined the fledgling organization.

Cooperation with four-year colleges: Several excellent examples of cooperation between community colleges and senior institutions were reported. These are found in California, Maryland, New York, Pennsylvania, and Washington.

Institutions of higher learning in the Baltimore, Maryland, area have joined together in the establishment of a Higher Education Council on Urban Affairs. The goal of the Council is to carry out on a continuing basis cooperative ventures in the areas of research, training, and action as they relate to urban problems. The Council is an outgrowth of two area-wide conferences sponsored by Essex Community College and funded by the Sears Roebuck Foundation. The purposes of the conferences were exchanging information, discussing needs and opportunities, and exploring the coordination of efforts relating to urban problems and social action.

An example of cooperation between a community college and a state college is the community development program funded under Title I of the Higher Education Act and carried out in Northern California. College of the Redwoods and Humboldt State College participated in the program in an extension of concerts and lecture series programs. Artists and lecturers were presented on campuses and in local communities.

Pasadena City College in California and the Western Center for Community Education and Development of the University of California Extension have cooperated in a program to train nonprofessional community aides as a part of the war on poverty. The pilot program conducted at Pasadena City College resulted in the development of an associate in arts degree program in community development and an in-service education program for already employed community aides in various antipoverty programs. As a result of the project, similar programs are being developed in other California junior colleges. The in-service education course is offered as a three-hour block once a week from 2:30 p.m. to 5:30 p.m. to allow agencies to release employees to take the course on company time.

Jamestown Community College in New York cooperated with Jamestown Business College, a private business school, in offering a short course in business communication for secretaries. The course was cosponsored by the local chapter of the National Secretaries Association. Thirty-nine enrolled for the ten-week program; the instructor was furnished by the business college.

The Community College of Philadelphia in Pennsylvania and thirty-six other two- and four-year colleges are participating in a consortium in the counseling area. The College Bound Corporation was developed to work in the high schools in the community two years ago at the initiative of the Community College of Philadelphia. The Corporation operates a central office and has a field staff of eight. Information regarding students counseled is filed centrally and transmitted to the individual colleges. Last year 1,000 interested students attended the Corporation's annual conference.

A most unique program known as Central Washington Adult Education for Migrants, to upgrade educational opportunities for migratory workers in a nine-county Washington area, was made possible when Big Bend Community College acquired a $700,000 grant from the Migrant Office of the Office of Educational Opportunity. The five-year program is being directed by Big Bend in cooperation with four other colleges and a school district. Organized as a college department within the General Education Division, CWAEM has its own director, an assistant for counseling, assistant director for curriculum, and a finance unit. The program, designed to bring migrants to a fifth-grade reading level, offers a prevocational exploratory program and then a vocational program, with the anticipated time sequence being two years from enrollment to an occupational skill.

Three New York community colleges, Nassau, Onondaga, Rockland; Queens College of the City University of New York; and six branches of the State University, Albany, Brockport, Buffalo, Fredonia, and Oswego, cooperate in offering credit telecourses of the University of The Air. Persons may enroll in the courses, which are broadcast over seven commercial stations on Saturdays at any of the institutions.

Two institutions of higher education, Seattle Community College and Washington State University, have joined forces in a cooperative extension service. Both seminars held as regular class sessions and television series are presented. Viewer's kits are mailed to registrants for use during television seminars.

A two-year study of the effects that dredging has on the marine life in estuarian areas has been a cooperative undertaking of four New York colleges: Suffolk County Community College, Fordham University, Hofstra University, and Southampton College. Scientists from the four colleges and marine technology students from Suffolk Community College are working on the Goose Creek Project on Long Island. The study was undertaken because estuarian areas are the base of the entire life cycle, yet no one is certain of the effects of dredging on these areas. Financed by a $75,000 grant from Suffolk County's Board of Supervisors, the project has developed new techniques of collecting quantitative samples of life from the bottom of estuaries, although it is still too early to predict outcomes of the research.

Cooperation with public schools: Rockland Community College in New York is the scene of the Rockland County Title III project, funded under the federal government's Elementary and Secondary Education Act of 1965. The project was initiated by the school executives of the county through an application forwarded by the Board of Cooperative Educational Services and is a joint effort by the public and private schools, colleges, and community agencies to improve education for all in the community. It seeks to enrich education in the county by making possible programs and services on a shared basis that would not otherwise be feasible. Although the college could not qualify under Title III, it can be a sponsoring and coordinating agency and is charged with general supervision and administration of all Title III activities. The director of the program is housed on the campus. Oakland Community College during the past year offered some eighty credit and noncredit courses in twenty-nine different centers in the college district in cooperation with local public schools.

Cooperation with community agencies: Santa Barbara City College has a long history of cooperation with community agencies in the sponsorship of all kinds of continuing education programs. The college has worked with seventy-six different Santa Barbara agencies to date in providing educational opportunities for adults.

CONCLUSION

The community college is the most rapidly growing element of higher education in America. The community services function, while still emerging as a major aspect of the program of these colleges, is the element that may best fit them for a unique and highly significant role in future patterns of American education.

Social, political, and economic trends clearly discernible throughout the country lend to the service program an importance that is growing daily. Both the growing recognition of the fact that to be educated, increasingly, means to continue to educate oneself, and the mushrooming demand of all sectors of American society for a meaningful education and a voice in educational policies, represent challenges which the community services operations of the community college are taking up. Unencumbered by a traditional format, concern with academic background and carry-over credits, and unhampered by powerful alumni forces devoted to the status quo, the community college itself has emerged in response to recognized community needs rather than to needs of a select class.

The community services program gives the community college its flexibility, its adaptability, its capability of providing education in whatever form and at whatever site necessary. By welcoming persons from all strata of the community and from both sides of the generation gap, the skilled and the unskilled, the cultured and the coarse, the educated and the illiterate, the community college chinks the educational panorama and offers enrichment to all citizens of its community.

More than other colleges, the community college is able to respond to problems of community life which, while not new, are newly acknowledged. Devoted to serving its locale, the community services program offers the logical vehicle for joining the college to the life of its district or service area. It is through the community services program that the college may not only offer educational programs and services needed in the community, utilize the total community as a laboratory-environment for learning, but may most readily draw the community itself into the process of shaping educational programs and policies. Programs designed by the college, based solely on the observations of its staff as to what is needed, run a high risk of being irrelevant to the most urgently felt needs of those for whom they are designed.

No aspect of any higher education program shares the ability of the community services programs to adopt to the changing milieu in which educational programs will be required to function. Because it represents not only a shift from the past, but a real adaption to the needs of the present and the future, the community services dimension of the community college will grow both in scope and importance in coming years.

Through its program of community services, the community college will insert into the life stream of its people forces that can change, revise, unify, and stimulate the individual, the organization, and ultimately, the tone of mind of the entire community.

SELECTED REFERENCES

1. Ashby, Sir Eric, "Higher Education in Tomorrow's World," *University of Michigan Sesquicentennial*, April 26–29, 1967.
2. Fusco, Gene C., "Telling the Story is Not Enough," *School Life*, XLIV (April 1962).
3. Gould, Samuel B., "Whose Goals for Higher Education?" remarks prepared for delivery before 50th Annual Meeting, American Council on Education, Washington, D.C., October 12, 1967.
4. Harlacher, Ervin L., "California's Community Renaissance," *Junior College Journal*, XXXIV (May 1964).
5. Harrington, Michael, *Taking A Great Society Seriously,* Harper's Magazine, Volume 233 (December 1966).
6. Havighurst, R. J., *Social and Cultural Changes Molding the Future of the American People.* Paper read at a UCEA Seminar at State University of New York at Buffalo, October, 1965.
7. Hutchins, Robert, Mimeographed statement. 1963.
8. Littlewood, Joan, "A Laboratory of Fun," *New Scientist*, Volume 22, May 14, 1964.
9. Mousolite, Peter S., *The Edge of the Chair*, remarks presented to National Conference on Vocational and Technical Education. Chicago: May 16, 1967.
10. Price, Cedric, "Potteries Thinkbelt," *New Society* (June 2, 1966).
11. Verner, Coolie, "The Junior College as a Social Institution," in Annual Florida Junior College Conference, *Community Services in the Community College*, Tallahassee, Florida State Department of Education, September 1960.
12. Weindenthal, Bud, *The Community College Commitment to the Inner City.* Washington, D.C.: American Association of Junior Colleges, 1967.

Appendix

A

RECOMMENDATIONS REGARDING THE ROLE OF THE AMERICAN ASSOCIATION OF JUNIOR COLLEGES IN THE DEVELOPMENT OF PROGRAMS OF COMMUNITY SERVICES[1]

I. Provide assistance in obtaining additional funds for community services
   —Provide clearinghouse on federal legislation relative to community services
   —Prepare publication of federal grants available for community services and criteria for programs
   —Provide assistance in developing proposals to federal agencies and private foundations
   —Lobby for additional federal support for community services
   —Promote inclusion of community services function in federal laws
   —Encourage state aid and local tax support for community services
   —Encourage foundation support for community services
   —Coordinate pilot programs in community services funded by federal or foundation grants
II. Support leadership training programs for community service personnel
   —Encourage leading universities to establish leadership training programs for community services personnel
   —Coordinate funding of experimental programs (field-based models and activities) in a number of selected community colleges in cooperation with University Leadership Training Programs

[1]Based on responses from sixty-five community college districts operating 104 college campuses in nineteen states.

—Provide in-service training programs in community services for selected professors in schools of education throughout the country

—Host a national conference on community services

—Encourage regional and statewide workshops and institutes on community services

III. Provide national clearinghouse on community service activities and studies

—Initiate more research studies on community services

—Disseminate information on a national scale

—Prepare and distribute publications on community services

—Publish monthly newsletter of activity in field

—Publish guidelines for establishing and strengthening program of community services

—Create idea bank

—Provide examples of community services programs being provided throughout the country

—Provide speakers, consultants, demonstrations, etc. when requested

—Provide assistance in evaluating community service programs

—Include more articles in the *Junior College Journal* on community services

IV. Contribute to understanding and support of community services as a major function

—Define the role and objectives of community services

—Recognize community services as major function of community college

—Provide vigorous leadership in strengthening and expanding community services programs

—Establish commission on community services

—Encourage commitment to community services on part of boards and top administrators

—Host planning meeting of community services leaders as means of following up current study

—Publish succinct position statement on community services function

—Add specialist on community services to A.A.J.C. staff to provide national leadership

—Encourage accreditation agencies to include community services as major area of investigation

—Promote development of national organization for community services personnel, either under aegis of A.A.J.C. or another appropriate association

Appendix

B

COMMUNITY COLLEGE DISTRICTS
VISITED DURING STUDY

Abraham Baldwin College, Georgia
Amarillo College, Texas
Baltimore Junior College, Maryland
Cabrillo College, California
Central Florida Junior College, Florida
Cerritos College, California
Chabot College, California
Chicago City College, Illinois
  Amundsen Campus
  Bogan Campus
  Crane Campus
  Fenger Campus
  Loop Campus
  Mayfair Campus
  Southeast Campus
  Wilson Campus
  Wright Campus
College of San Mateo, California
Community College of Philadelphia, Pennsylvania
Cuyahoga Community College, Ohio
  Metropolitan Campus
  Western Campus
Del Mar College, Texas
Delta College, Michigan

El Centro College, Texas
Essex Community College, Maryland
Flint Community Junior College, Michigan
Foothill Junior College District, California
  DeAnza College
  Foothill College
Jamestown Community College, New York
Junior College District of St. Louis, Missouri
  Florissant Valley Community College
  Forest Park Community College
  Meramac Community College
Kellogg Community College, Michigan
Los Angeles Junior College District, California
  East Los Angeles College
  Los Angeles City College
  Los Angeles Harbor College
  Los Angeles Pierce College
  Los Angeles Southwest College
  Los Angeles Trade-Technical College
  Los Angeles Valley College
Los Rios Junior College District, California
  American River College
  Sacramento City College
Miami-Dade Junior College, Florida
  North Campus
  South Campus
Milwaukee Institute of Technology, Wisconsin
Monterey Peninsula College, California
Montgomery Junior College, Maryland
  Rockville Campus
  Tacoma Park Campus
New York City Community College, New York
North Florida Junior College, Florida
Oakland Community College, Michigan
  Auburn Hills Campus
  Highland Lakes Campus
  Orchard Ridge Campus
Peralta Junior College District, California
  Laney College
  Merritt College

Rockland Community College, New York
San Antonio Junior College District, Texas
  San Antonio College
  St. Phillip's College
San Jose City College, California
Santa Fe Junior College, Florida
State University of New York Agricultural & Technical College at
  Farmingdale, New York
Suffolk County Community College, New York
Westark Junior College, Arkansas

Appendix

C

COMMUNITY COLLEGE DISTRICTS
CORRESPONDED WITH DURING STUDY

Bakersfield College, California
Big Bend Community College, Washington
Bucks County Community College, Pennsylvania
College of the Redwoods, California
Community College of Allegheny County, Pennsylvania
    Allegheny Campus
    East Campus
Daytona Beach Junior College, Florida
El Camino College, California
Essex County College, New Jersey
Harrisburg Area Community College, Pennsylvania
Hudson Valley Community College, New York
Long Beach City College, California
Macomb County Community College, Michigan
    Center Campus
    South Campus
Mira Costa College, California
Mt. San Antonio College, California
Northern Virginia Community College, Virginia
Orange Coast Junior College District, California
    Golden West College
    Orange Coast College
Orange County Community College, New York

Pasadena City College, California
Portland Community College, Oregon
Prairie State College, Illinois
Rock Valley College, Illinois
Roger Williams College, Rhode Island
San Bernardino Valley College, California
Santa Barbara City College, California
Santa Monica City College, California
St. Petersburg Junior College, Florida
   Clearwater Campus
   St. Petersburg Campus
Seattle Community College, Washington
Vincennes University Junior College, Indiana

Appendix

D

CHECK LIST FOR
EFFECTIVE PROGRAMS
OF COMMUNITY SERVICES

The effective administration and supervision of the program of community services involves:

I. Securing community-college support
   A. Involve community in planning and development
      —Utilize personnel of appropriate community groups in planning and promotion of program
      —Engage community advisory committees in planning of program
      —Obtain cosponsorship of services and activities by local groups
      —Actively involve a large number of community people and groups in program
      —Secure active participation and support of community leaders
      —Organize community advisory council as means of identifying community needs and interests
      —Develop and maintain cooperative, friendly relationships with community groups
      —Arrange for community cultural groups to affiliate with college
   B. Maintain effective internal and external communication
      —Establish regular information service to keep citizens of college district community informed on college matters
      —Provide adequate time to plan publicity campaigns
      —Use a wide variety of media to communicate with public and reach all segments of college district community

—Direct publicity and publications toward specific audiences in community

—Utilize extensive direct mail publicity

—Arrange for direct coverage of college events by area press

—Develop and maintain personal relationship with area press

—Prepare brochures regarding activities and services and distribute throughout community

—Issue personal invitations to community leaders to attend events

—Keep public fully informed of services available from college

—Establish citizens' committees as an aid in presenting programs to community

—Clarify channels of communication between community services office and other college departments involved in providing services

C. Involve faculty and students in planning and development

—Encourage active participation of faculty and students in program

—Organize student-faculty planning committee

—Provide opportunity for faculty to help plan program informally and through study and advisory committees

D. Coordinate services with other community groups

—Coordinate program with other community and regional groups to avoid unnecessary duplication of services

—Maintain close liaison with public school personnel of college district

—Encourage communitywide coordination of cultural and recreational activities

E. Encourage college staff to participate in community affairs

—Encourage college personnel to participate in community activities

—Make college personnel available to community as consultants

—Provide leadership in organizing needed community groups and solving community problems

F. Orient faculty and staff to community service function

—Interpret community service function to college faculty and staff on continuous basis

II. Determining nature and scope of program

A. Provide effective planning and research

—Insure long-range planning of program

—Plan carefully all details of each individual service or activity

—Begin planning of individual services and activities at early date

—Consider carefully timing of services or activities
—Encourage staff experimentation and innovation in developing program
—Invite community groups to utilize college facilities and resources
—Preplan advisory committee meetings carefully
—Obtain evaluation of services and activities from participants
—Conduct appropriate research studies, including surveys and polls

B. Establish high standards for public performance
—Select known, quality artists and lecturers
—Determine and adhere to standards for public performance

C. Tailor services to specific needs and interests
—Tailor program and individual services to meet needs and interests of specific groups in district community

D. Define program purposes and objectives
—Determine objectives and philosophy of program and individual services
—Emphasize educational aspects of program
—Present diversified and balanced program
—Define specific functions of citizens' advisory committees

E. Identify community needs and interests
—Make community survey to determine specific needs and interests of district community
—Base each decision to provide a service or activity on analysis of community needs and interests
—Hold conferences and informal discussions with community people for purposes of determining community needs and interests
—Encourage community-at-large to express its desires and needs for specific services

III. Organizing and administering program

A. Provide effective administration and supervision
—Establish community services division as major administrative area
—Obtain full-time community services administrator to provide leadership and assume over-all responsibility for program
—Provide adequate staff to organize and implement program
—Select enthusiastic, well-qualified staff supervisors for program
—Employ qualified public information officer
—Provide supervisors with sufficient time and authority to plan and coordinate activities

—Assure staff supervisors of freedom and authority to develop their activities

—Obtain adequate clerical assistance

—Select membership of citizens' advisory committees carefully on basis of purposes of committee

—Provide expert staff help for citizens' advisory groups

—Provide over-all coordination of events cosponsored by community groups

B. Establish and adhere to written policies, regulations, and procedures

—Establish written policies, regulations, and procedures for all aspects of program

—Apply policies and regulations uniformly

—Review policies, regulations, and procedures periodically to see if they are still effective

—Maintain flexibility in accommodating community needs

—Require that all instructions and requirements for use of college facilities be in writing

—Arrange meeting with representatives of groups using college facilities for detailed joint-planning

—Require college supervisor to be present during time facility is being used by community group

C. Utilize community facilities and resources

—Offer services and activities at off-campus locations

—Utilize qualified consultants in developing program when need arises

D. Secure board, administration, and faculty support

—Secure understanding and support of board of trustees for program

—Elicit support and cooperation of administration and faculty

—Obtain support of board, administration, and faculty for community service as a major function

E. Obtain essential resources

—Secure essential financial support for program

—Provide adequate facilities and equipment for program[1]

[1]Ervin L. Harlacher, *Effective Junior College Programs of Community Services: Rationale, Guidelines, Practices.* Junior College Leadership Program, Occasional Report Number 10. Los Angeles: School of Education, University of California, 1967.

Appendix
E

ADDITIONAL NOTEWORTHY
COMMUNITY SERVICE PROGRAMS
IN COMMUNITY COLLEGES

I. Community Use of College Facilities and Services

A. Noncredit Short Courses:

1. Among colleges that have given particular attention to noncredit short courses is Abraham Baldwin Agricultural College in Georgia. Since 1940, the college has offered a series of short courses for Georgia farmers, stressing latest techniques in farming and related fields. Courses are usually for one day only—occasionally two—concentrate on one facet of a given topic, are tailored to fit expressed needs, and offered without charge except for cost of food when served.

In twenty-seven years, 743 short courses have been offered with a total of nearly 100,000 people in attendance. These people came from 153 of Georgia's 159 counties, thirty-six states plus the District of Columbia, and thirty-seven foreign countries as far apart as Korea and South Africa, England, and Thailand.

Other organizations that cooperated with the college in the program are Georgia's Coastal Plain Experiment Station, Agricultural Extension Service, Department of Vocational Education, the Soil Conservation Service, Farmer's Home Administration, the U.S. Department of Agriculture, outstanding farmers, and commercial firms.

Ten advisory committees work with the college in developing the series. There are committees on agricultural engineering, agronomy, animal husbandry, business, conservation, economics and farm management, forestry, horticulture, poultry, and activities of rural women. Advisory committees hold an annual all-day meeting in May to plan the following year's program.

2. Short courses designed for a metropolitan population have been developed by Milwaukee Institute of Technology.

An Institute and Clinic program in 1966–67 presented 127 short courses to 31,160 persons. The program began twenty-three years ago with a sales clinic for about fifty sales and marketing personnel. The 127 institutes were cosponsored by the college and seventy-nine Milwaukee area organizations representing business, industry, labor, education, and government. One hundred seventy speakers were engaged for the noncredit courses. Some of the speakers came from outside the metropolitan area and a few were members of the college faculty.

Much of the instruction is provided by the cosponsoring agencies without cost to the college. Some college staff members serve without pay. Most courses are a single session; maximum is three sessions.

Ideas for seminars come from members of civic, business, industrial, or professional organizations, and the faculty. Each program lists the college as a cosponsor and is open to the public and free. Promotional flyers are created for each program.

Objectives of the program include the provision of sound educational programs for Milwaukee area business, industry, and homemakers; the opportunity to exchange ideas, experiences, and opinions; and the stimulation of persons to more effective performance on their jobs. One of the greatest objectives is to further cooperation between Milwaukee Institute of Technology, area business, government, industry, management, labor, and the home.

B. In-service Training:

1. Del Mar College in Texas has developed in-service training programs for business, industry, and trades.

In the area of business, Del Mar mails out a monthly registration schedule to persons interested in courses offered in its department of sales and marketing. These include courses in advertising, general business, hotel-motel management, insurance, real estate, salesmanship, and courses of special interest that are applicable to the entire business community. Ninety to 100 courses are offered each year to an annual enrollment of approximately 3,000. The minimum is fifteen students per class and classes may meet at any place that is convenient to the group and where satisfactory arrangements can be made. For example, classes have been held on campus, at department stores, milk companies, hotels, and motels. The food service management series, designed for those currently employed or contemplating employment in the food service industry, is offered at local motels or hotels for a full semester, two hours per day, two days a week.

The college's trade and industrial extension program is another offering that attracts large numbers of students. The program is designed to upgrade the trades by providing in-service training for persons currently employed. Classes average fifteen students each. Most of the courses run on a semester basis. Some are shorter. Subject matter is tailored to student needs and all instructors come from industry. Enrollment in the total program in 1966–67 was 2,700. It offered eighty-one noncredit courses in the fall, a total of 186 for the year, primarily on the technical institute campus. A few apprentice training programs are offered in-plant. The college is classified as an area vocational school, but it may not enroll any student who is enrolled in high school. For this reason, the average age of enrollees is about thirty.

The program director believes the absence of credit is an asset. "Our purpose is to upgrade a man's skills," he explains, "so we can begin working with him wherever he is. If the students were being offered credit, unrelated theory would have to be covered and we could not do as good a job." Students receive certificates for eighty percent attendance, and in the majority of cases industry reimburses them for the tuition if the course is satisfactorily completed.

C. Community Counseling:

1. North Florida Junior College has provided the leadership for the development of guidance services for elementary schools, high schools, and junior colleges in six rural counties.

The college took the lead in the development of guidance services for elementary schools, high schools, and junior colleges in the rural counties. An area Guidance Center was organized in July 1959 to serve high schools in five counties. By 1965 it extended to a sixth county and included elementary and vocational schools and junior colleges. Prior to 1959 none of these schools had any organized guidance service. Now all meet state accreditation standards for guidance. Twenty counselors provide 115 hours of guidance time daily.

The Center makes a number of services available to area counselors. Eight one-day workshops are offered per year, with cooperating superintendents and principals providing release time to enable attendance by their part-time counselors. The Center also distributes guidance films, filmstrips, tapes, books, and mimeographed materials for use by faculty and students.

An area testing program is a cooperative effort of participating schools. The Guidance Center processes the answer sheets, makes the statistical computations, and distributes results to all schools. Participating counties pay the yearly rental of the IBM scoring machine. Additional cooperative efforts are school and area follow-up studies, research projects undertaken with the help of two state universities, and participation in a pilot project of data-processing student records and transcripts.

Federal funds under the National Defense Education Act, Title V-A, provided seed money for the Center. The bountiful crop is provided by local expenditure for guidance. The Center maintains contact with agencies under the Economic Opportunity Act, and with the Rural Development Council and the state employment agencies.

2. An outstanding community counseling program is in evidence at Rockland Community College in New York.

Organized in 1966, the New York State Guidance Center for Women is sponsored by the State University of New York and Rockland Community College. During its first year, the Center served 365 clients in counseling and testing in addition to approximately 175 others who received direct service from the library or other informational services. Women served so far fall into the middle levels of educational and socioeconomic backgrounds, but it is anticipated that the proportion will increase at the lower levels as the outreach counseling services are expanded in low income areas. Most of the women are in their thirties and early forties, needing counseling to help guide them in their choice of vocational goals.

Individual guidance and counseling is carried on by a staff of trained professionals, each of whom has at least a master's degree in counseling or guidance and related experience with adults. In addition, there is group counseling with small numbers of individuals who share a common interest. As an integral part of the counseling, vocational and educational testing is used. Group guidance workshops are focused on the social skills involved in career exploration and progress. Lectures and discussions are planned by representatives of business, industry, and the professions in which requirements, duties, and current issues in their particular specialties are covered. An up-to-date library is maintained in which vocational and educational information on specific fields in the local and metropolitan area, as well as general opportunities and resources, is available. In order to serve all individuals in the community, the Center fills requests to take its services to groups of individuals who would have difficulty in coming to the Center, characteristically into low income areas. Radio programs are also presented by representatives of business, industry, or the professions dealing with the requirements, duties, and current trends in employment in their areas.

The staff of the Guidance Center works with both a community advisory committee, representing area employers and educational institutions, and a state advisory committee composed of state leaders in business, industry, the professions, and education.

D. Human Resource Development:

1. New York City Community College has found an effective means of developing the undeveloped talents and job potential of Brooklyn's disadvantaged young people.

Its Urban Center program helps prepare high school graduates in the lower quarter of the class for job training and placement. The Center offers five programs: office skills, secretarial science, drafting, business machine repair, and college adapter. Two programs are to be added to accommodate dropouts: route merchandising and laundry apparel processing.

Established in September, 1966, the Urban Center is one of four centers for which the State Legislature appropriated funds through the State University of New York.

Of 40 students enrolled initially in the office skills program, thirty-one, or seventy-seven percent, completed the first cycle of classes. Of the forty, all but four were either placed in full-time employment or continued their educations, either at the Urban Center or by entering regular programs of New York City Community College. Later courses had an even higher retention rate. In the fall of 1967 enrollment was 396 in the five programs. Courses varied in length from six months to a year. Although the programs were originally developed for those with a high school diploma or a General Equivalency Diploma, new courses are being added for dropouts. In order to be eligible for the program, students must be financially unable to attend a private educational institution.

The Center is open from 8:00 a.m. to 6:00 p.m. Recruitment is handled through high school counselors, community agencies, and walk-ins. The ratio of students to counselors is fifty to one, and for the placement office, the ratio is 200 to one. Each student spends from twenty-two to thirty-two hours per week at the Center. Those in the skills programs have employment placement guaranteed.

Admission to the college adapter program is based on testing and counseling. Three recommendations from the high school are required as well as up to three different interviews by counselors.

Evening programs are planned in the skill areas for adults, and individual study in the program is being emphasized through some use of multimedia.

2. Project SERVE of Oakland Community College, Michigan, provides counseling services for senior citizens.

Project SERVE (Stimulate, Educate, Reassess, Volunteer, and Employ) was initiated in 1966. It provides free counseling and placement for senior citizens needing additional income. It operates a volunteer placement bureau to utilize the reservoir of talent and experience of the community's older citizens and it provides new sources of participation and stimulation through short courses tailored specifically for their needs.

Approximately half of the initial roster of senior citizens interviewed have been placed in jobs, varying from janitor to a tutor of adult illiterates. Current expansion of the list of senior citizens with specific qualifications for which jobs are available is under way as well as finding jobs for those senior citizens now on the roster.

For senior citizens who have no financial need, varied volunteer assignments are of service to social agencies. Such activities include the care of young children at a local agency, serving as case aides to the elderly, providing transportation to clinics, serving as program consultant for Scout troops, participating in outdoor education and camping programs, and providing clerical assistance.

Courses devised specifically for senior citizens include symposiums based on the theme, "Challenge of Change and New Trends in Education"; a workshop in "New Dimensions"; a series entitled "Don't Let Your Money Retire," covering frauds, quackery, consumer traps, nutrition, etc.; and a course in "Leadership Training."

Plans for the future included formation of a dramatic group, creation of a newspaper that would provide a master calendar of senior citizen events, a health forum, courses in estate planning, human relations, personal problems, and hobbies for profit, and a series of forums on points of disagreement between generations.

E. Campus Radio-Television Station:

1. Students at Long Beach City College in California assist in the operation and maintenance of "Radio KLON, the Station of the Public Schools," which serves 100,000 elementary and secondary students annually.

On the air daily throughout the school year, this noncommercial FM station has its studios located on the campus of Long Beach City College in the Business and Technology Division. It is owned and operated by the Long Beach Unified School District. Cultural and scientific information is provided for kindergarten through twelfth-grade students. Intradistrict communication is another function with talks from the superintendent to teachers in the seventy-nine schools at a time to coincide with faculty meetings.

Many of the station's programs are written and produced by the KLON staff to meet the special curricular needs of the district. Others are procured from the National Association of Educational Broadcasters of which Long Beach Unified School District is a member. The station staff cooperates with the Los Angeles County Division of Radio-TV Education to provide additional programming.

2. Chicago City College operates a TV college as part of its service to residents of the surrounding area enabling them to take courses at home, either for credit or noncredit. TV College is the open-circuit extension of the Chicago City College, and is on the air about twenty-six hours per week. More than seventy different courses have been offered and since 1956 almost 170,000 enrollments have been completed by 100,000 persons. About 140 of these students have completed all the work required for the Associate in Arts degree. Some seventy-five percent of the home viewers who enroll for credit complete their courses. And, because TV College does not compromise its standards, these students are able to transfer units to other colleges and universities and compete successfully with those educated in an on-campus situation.

One reason for the success of its students is the high calibre of the faculty. About one-half hold the Ph.D. degree. As a group they average ten-and-a-half years' teaching experience at the college level. They are screened and selected for television teaching on the basis of teaching skill.

To assure ample time for careful course planning, each teacher is hired two months at full pay for course preparation and development of study guides and instructional materials, usually in the summer preceding his live presentation. In addition, he is released from all other duties during the term of live teaching in order to prepare and present two forty-five minute telecasts per week.

The TV program started on an experimental basis in 1956, underwritten partly by a three-year, $500,000 grant from the Fund for the Advancement of Education and partly by matching funds from the Chicago Board of Education. In 1959 it was made a regular service of what was then known as Chicago City Junior College and was entirely supported by the taxpayers through their common schools until 1965. At that time TV College became part of a reorganized junior college system now known as Chicago City College and governed by its own board. Studio facilities are rented from the local educational television station.

II. Community Development

A. Organization of Community Councils, Coordinating Councils, and Other Needed Community Agencies and Groups:

1. Educational administrators of the six counties joined with North Florida Junior College to establish the Area Audio-Visual Materials Center for pooling of materials to improve instruction in mathematics, science and language.

It is well-stocked with materials in the natural sciences; current buying will be devoted to social studies and languages. The current selection of materials, valued at more than $100,000, includes some 550 films as well as filmstrips, slides, pictures, models, tapes, recordings, charts, graphs, special science equipment, and other A-V materials.

The Center began in 1960 as a project under the National Defense Education Act funded on a fifty-fifty basis. The county school system contributes 15 cents for each of the 16,000 students in grades one to twelve in the forty-five schools serviced, based on average daily attendance. Administrative costs are paid by the college. Policy and purchases are determined by a board whose membership includes the supervisor of instructional materials from each county system and the NFJC director of library services. A part-time director operates the Center, which is housed in the NFJC library building.

The Center offers quick service and low cost. Shipment takes place within 24 hours and the only expense for the school utilizing the materials is return postage. There is no rental fee. The Center services its own material. During the 1966–67 college year withdrawals totaled more than 1,400 films and a 20 percent increase was expected for 1967–68. The Area Audio-Visual Materials Center is rendering service to the multicounty participants that would not be available to them on their individual shoestring contributions.

2. Oakland County Police Academy was organized by Oakland Community College, Michigan, to fill a community need.

The Academy was established on the Auburn Hills campus of Oakland Community College in March, 1967, culminating many months of work by the Oakland County Law Enforcement Committee to increase the number of meaningful police training programs in the area. Within six months from the time the college officials were first contacted, the first Basic Police Training Course had a graduating class of forty-five police trainees.

The Academy has a twenty-five member advisory committee composed of representatives of all county law enforcement agencies, which works closely with the college in determining courses, curriculum, instructors, rules, and policies of the Academy. Specialized short courses were offered during the summer of 1967 and ten short courses, in addition to the Basic Police Training Program, were scheduled for the 1967–68 academic year covering such subjects as accident investigation, police instructor training, accident records, traffic law enforcement, in-service refresher, police supervision, riot control, and investigative techniques.

Police training offered at the Academy is meeting a very definite need of law enforcement agencies in the Oakland-Wayne-Macomb tri-county area. Through initiative and sheer persistence, the college, joining forces with county law enforcement agencies to form the first training center of this kind in the country, has within one year attained goals that many said could not be accomplished.

III. Cultural and Recreational Activities

A. Arts, Lectures, and Film Series:

1. Flint Community Junior College, Michigan, held a seminar in arts titled "The Search for Meaning in the Arts."

The purpose of the seminar was to explore, through the mutual exchange of ideas and attitudes, what an audience can expect from a work of art and what "meaning" can imply to a viewer of a painting or play, an individual listening to music, or a reader of a book. There were no speeches and no presentations of formal papers.

Twenty-five persons participated in 1967 at a cost of $20 each. They included seven college staff members from art, music, drama, and literature, and eighteen community persons in response to a personal invitation. The seminar ran a day-and-a-half.

Besides stimulating interest in the arts, the seminar helped to demonstrate to status individuals in the community the quality of the college staff and to help move the staff into additional contact with the community. Participants were enthusiastic about the seminar and plans were made to make it an annual affair, extending it to include a student group and a teacher group.

B. Community Performing Groups:

1. Flint Community Junior College, Michigan, offers an annual summer theater program employing a professional resident theater company averaging about thirty members.

The ten-week program is heavily subsidized by private, institutional, and corporate philanthropy. About 75 percent of the program costs are covered by the contributions of F. A. Bower (for whom the theater is named), Flint Community Junior College, the committee of Sponsors of Flint's College and Cultural Center, the IBM Corporation, and Professional Theatre of Flint. The balance is provided by income from ticket sales. The heavy subsidization makes possible a low admission charge, which encourages student and total community attendance.

Summer, 1967, saw the presentation of four plays, *A Thurber Carnival, Tobacco Road, Ah Wilderness!,* and *The Night of the Iguana,* each having a two-week run.

Several key production and administrative positions are filled by members of the college's regular theater staff and its equipment and theater are used. In addition, actors and production personnel are employed from many other parts of the country for the summer with theater students from Flint Community Junior College and University of Michigan, Flint College employed as apprentices. The student body benefits from having a high quality theater program available at low cost and the experience of working with a professional company. In addition the program has made a substantial contribution to the cultural life of the Flint community.

Selected Community Services Bibliography

A. BOOKS

Barr, Arvil S., Robert A. Davis, and Palmer O. Johnson, *Educational Research and Appraisal*. Chicago: J. B. Lippincott Company, 1953.

Bogue, Jess, *The Community College*. New York: McGraw-Hill, 1950.

Brownell, Baker, *The College and the Community*. New York: Harper & Brothers, 1952.

——, *The Human Community*. New York: Harper & Brothers, 1959.

Campbell, Ronald F., and John A. Ramseyer, *The Dynamics of School Community Relationships*. New York: Allyn and Bacon, 1955.

Clark, Burton R., *Adult Education in Transition: A Study of Institutional Insecurity*. Berkeley, Calif.: University of California Press, 1958.

——, *Educating the Expert Society*. San Francisco, Calif.: Chandler Publishing Company, 1962.

Dyer, John P., *Ivory Towers in the Market Place*. New York: Bobbs-Merrill Company, 1956.

Fields, Ralph R., *The Community College Movement*. New York: McGraw-Hill, 1952.

Flanagan, John C., et. al., *Critical Requirements for Research Personnel*. Pittsburg, Pa.: American Institute for Research, 1949.

Gleazer, Edmund J., Jr., ed., *An Introduction to Junior Colleges*. Washington, D.C.: American Association of Junior Colleges, 1960.

Good, Carter V., *Introduction to Educational Research*. New York: Appleton-Century-Crofts, Inc., 1963.

Grinnell, J. E., and Raymond J. Young, *The School and the Community*. New York: The Ronald Press Company, 1955.

Hamlin, Herbert M., *Citizens' Committees in the Public Schools*. Danville, Ill.: The Interstate Printers and Publishers, 1952.

130

Harlacher, Ervin L., *Effective Junior College Programs of Community Services*: *Rationale, Guidelines, Practices*. Junior College Leadership Program, Occasional Report No. 10, Los Angeles: University of California, Los Angeles, 1967.

Henry, Nelson B., ed., *The Public Junior College*. 55th Yearbook, National Society for the Study of Education. Chicago: The University of Chicago Press, 1956.

Hillway, Tyrus, *The American Two-Year College*. New York: Harper & Brothers, 1958.

Holy, T. C., and H. H. Semans, *A Restudy of the Needs of California in Higher Education*. Sacramento, Calif.: California State Department of Education, 1956.

Knowles, Malcolm S., *The Adult Education Movement in the United States*. New York: Holt, Rinehart and Winston, 1962.

Lackey, Katherine, *Community Development Through University Extension*. Community Development Publication No. 3. Carbondale, Ill.: Southern Illinois University, 1960.

Medsker, Leland, *The Junior College: Progress and Prospect*. New York: McGraw-Hill, 1960.

Morton, John R., *University Extension in the United States*. University, Ala.: University of Alabama Press, 1953.

National Education Association, Department of Elementary School Principals, *How to Know and How to Use Your Community*. Washington, D.C.: The Association, 1941–1942.

Pierce, Truman, Edward G. Merrill, Craig Wilson, and Ralph B. Kimbrough, *Community Leadership for Public Education*. Englewood Cliffs, N.J.: Prentice-Hall, Inc., 1955.

Price, Hugh G., *California Public Junior Colleges*. Sacramento: California State Department of Education, 1958.

Punke, Harold H., *Community Use of School Facilities*. New York: King's Crown Press, 1951.

Reeder, Ward G., *An Introduction to Public-School Relations*. New York: The Macmillan Company, 1953.

Reynolds, James W., *An Analysis of Community Service Programs of Junior Colleges*. Washington, D.C.: U.S. Office of Education, 1960.

Ryans, David G., *Characteristics of Teachers*. Washington, D.C.: American Council on Education, 1960.

Seay, Maurice F., and Ferris N. Crawford, *The Community School and Community Self-Improvement*. Lansing, Mich.: Clair L. Taylor, Superintendent of Public Instruction, 1954.

Sheats, Paul, Clarence D. Jayne, and Ralph B. Spence, *Adult Education*. New York: The Dryden Press, 1953.

Stearns, Harry L., *Community Relations and the Public Schools*. Englewood Cliffs, N. J.: Prentice-Hall, Inc., 1955.

Thelen, Herbert A., *Dynamics of Groups at Work*. Chicago: The University of Chicago Press, 1954.

Thornton, James W., Jr., *The Community Junior College*. New York: John Wiley and Sons, 1960.

Whitlaw, John B., *The School and Its Community*. Baltimore, Md.: The Johns Hopkins Press, 1951.

B. PERIODICALS

Bard, Harry, Leon R. Learner, and Leona S. Morris, "Operation: Collegiate Horizons," *Junior College Journal*, XXXVIII (September 1967), 16–21.

Barnes, John B., "The Community College's Newest Obligation," *Junior College Journal*, XXVIII (January 1958), 247–50.

Basler, Roosevelt, "Consistent and Increasing Adaptability of the Junior College," *Junior College Journal*, XXV (April 1955), 427–29.

Bevlin, Marjorie, "The Junior College as a Community Art Center," *Junior College Journal* XXX (April 1960), 442–45.

Corbally, John E., Jr., "The Critical Incident Technique and Educational Research," *Educational Research Bulletin*, XXXV (March 14, 1956), 57–62.

——, "A Second Look at the Critical Incident Technique," *Phi Delta Kappan*, XXXVIII (January 1957), 141–42.

Donham, Dan J., "We Can Serve Welfare Recipients," *Junior College Journal*, XXXVIII (March 1968), 74–76.

Fusco, Gene C., "Telling the School Story is Not Enough," *School Life*, XLIV (April 1962), 9–12.

Gleazer, Edmund J., Jr., "AAJC Approach: Summer Community Services," *Junior College Journal*, XXXVIII (March 1968), 9.

Gordon, Thomas, "The Use of the Critical Incident Technique in Construction of an Evaluation Procedure for Airline Pilots," *American Psychologist*, IV (July 1949), 301.

Halfter, Irma T., "The Comparative Academic Achievement of Women," *Adult Education*, XII (Winter 1962), 106–15.

Harlacher, Ervin L., "California's Community Renaissance," *Junior College Journal*, XXXIV (May 1964).

——, "Effective Educational Public Relations Begin at Home," *Junior College Journal*, XXXI (September 1960), 25–30.

——, "New Directions in Community Services," *Junior College Journal*, XXXVIII (March 1968), 12–17.

Houle, Cyril O., "Community Educational Service: An Emerging Function of Higher Education," *Proceedings of the Institute for Administrative Officers of Higher Institutions* (1948), 5–13.

——, "The Obligation of the Junior College for Community Service," *Junior College Journal*, XXX (May 1960), 502–16.

Hudson, Roy F., "Increasing College-Community Activities," *Junior College Journal*, XXIX (November 1958), 153–55.

Jensen, A. C., "Determining Critical Requirements for Teachers," *Journal of Experimental Education*, XX (September 1951), 79–85.

Johnson, B. Lamar, "Is the Junior College Idea Useful for Other Countries?" *Junior College Journal* XXXI (September 1961), 3–8.

——, "The Junior College: Its Role and Its Future," *Phi Delta Kappan*, XXXVIII (February 1957), 182–86.

Judd, Robert C., "Needed: Three Vice Presidents," *College and University Business*, XXIX (November 1960), 32–35.

Kaplan, Abbot, "Fifth Dimension in American Education: Adult Education," *Educational Forum*, XXVI (1962), 133–42.

Koch, Moses S., and Saul E. Libenstein, "A Community College Attracts the Aging," *Junior College Journal*, XXXV (October 1964), 26–27.

Koch, Moses S., and Priscilla M. Wolley, "Established: A Curriculum to Train Urban Professional Assistants," *Junior College Journal*, XXXVIII (October 1967), 20–24.

Menefee, Audrey G., "There's a Meeting Here Tonight," *Junior College Journal*, XXXI (March 1961), 387–90.

——, "The Community Survey: First Step for a New College," *Junior College Journal*, XXVIII (1958), 259–61.

Newman, Fred M., and Donald W. Oliver, "Education and Community," *Harvard Educational Review*, XXXVII (Winter 1967), 61–106.

Padrow, Ben, "Community College: A Dramatic Conception," *Junior College Journal*, XXVIII (September 1957), 44–46.

Putnam, Howard, "The College Community-Service Program as an Agency of Social Action," *Junior College Journal*, XXXI (December 1960), 221–23.

Reynolds, James W., "Community Colleges and Studies of Communities," *Junior College Journal*, XXXI (October 1960), 63–64.

Rollins, Charles E., and Wallace B. Appleson, "Accent on a Cultural Commitment," *Junior College Journal*, XXXVIII (October 1967), 30–31.

Stapley, Maurice E., and Harlan Beem, "Effective Board Functioning," *School Executive*, LXXIII (March 1954), 101–3.

Steinberg, Sheldon S., and Eunice O. Shatz, "Junior Colleges and the New Careers Program," *Junior College Journal*, XXXVIII (February 1968), 12–17.

Vaccaro, Louis C., "The Manpower Development and Training Act and the Community College," *Junior College Journal*, XXXIV (November 1963), 21–23.

Waggoner, Ann Carr, "Venture Into Continuing Education," *Junior College Journal*, XXX (September 1960), 44–49.

Wagner, Ralph W., "Using Critical Incidents to Determine Test Weights," *Personnel Psychology*, IV (Winter 1951), 373–81.

Woods, Thomas E., "Community Development—3rd Phase of the Junior College Movement," *Junior College Journal*, XXVII (September 1956), 42–47.

C. REPORTS

American Association of Junior Colleges, Commission on Legislation, *Establishing Legal Bases for Community Colleges*. Proceedings of a conference, October 20–21, 1961. Washington, D.C.: The Association, n.d.

Harlacher, Ervin L., *A Program of Community Services for Cerritos College*. Community Services Study Report No. V. Norwalk, Calif.: Cerritos College, June 1964.

——, *The Community Dimension of the Community College*, Washington, D.C. The American Association of Junior Colleges, November, 1967.

Johnson, B. Lamar, chm., "How to Appraise Public Service," A Report of Study Committee No. 4. *How to Appraise the Value of the University to Society*. Ninth all-university faculty conference. Berkeley, Calif.: University of California, 1954.

Verner, Coolie, "The Junior College as a Social Institution," *Community Services in the Community Junior Colleges*. Proceedings of the Annual Florida Junior College Conference. Tallahassee, Fla.: Florida State Department of Education, September 1960.

D. UNPUBLISHED MATERIALS

Adams, Robert Cay, *Development of the Community and Extension Program for the Schools of Arizona*. Unpublished Master's thesis, School of Education, Stanford University, 1936.

Barnhart, Richard E., *The Critical Requirements for School Board Membership Based Upon an Analysis of Critical Incidents*. Unpublished Ed.D. dissertation, Indiana University, 1952.

Benson, Ellis M., *A Time and Sequence Analysis of Critical Steps in the Establishment of California Public Junior Colleges*. Unpublished Ed.D. dissertation, University of California, Los Angeles, 1963.

Blank, Lane B., *A Study of Critical Incidents in the Behavior of Secondary Physical Education Instructors*. Unpublished Ed.D. dissertation, University of California, Los Angeles, 1957.

Corbally, John E., Jr., *A Study of the Critical Elements of School Board-Community Relations*. Unpublished Ph.D. dissertation, University of California, Berkeley, 1955.

Cruzen-Loder, Eugenia, *The Community College: A Program of Community Participation in Education.* Unpublished Ed.D. dissertation, Stanford University, 1955.

Fails, Emil, *The Potential Role of Public Community Junior Colleges.* Unpublished Ph.D. dissertation, George Peabody College for Teachers, 1956.

Harlacher, Ervin L., *Community Services in California Public Junior Colleges.* Unpublished study, School of Education, Stanford University, 1960.

———, *Critical Requirements for the Establishment of Effective Junior College Programs of Community Services.* Unpublished Ed.D. dissertation, University of California, Los Angeles, 1965.

Jones, Bertis L., *The History of Community Development in American Universities With Particular Reference to Four Selected Institutions* Unpublished Ed.D. dissertation, 1961.

———, *The Status of Community Development in the United States.* Unpublished report based on a survey of 75 National University Extension Association Institutions, 1957.

McDaniel, Lucy V., *Critical Behavior of Staff Physical Therapists.* Unpublished Ed.D. dissertation, University of California, Los Angeles, 1961.

MacGilvra, Donald Everett, *A Study of the Community Service Programs of the Business Administration Departments of the Public Community Junior Colleges of the State of Washington.* Unpublished Master's thesis, School of Education, University of Washington, 1959.

Pfeiffer, Clyde Emmett, *An Attitudinal Study of the Educational Program at John Muir College,* Unpublished Ed.D. dissertation, University of California, Los Angeles, 1950.

Richards, Jerrel T., *Critical Incidents in the Orientation of Newly Appointed Junior College Instructors.* Unpublished Ed.D. dissertation, University of California, Los Angeles, 1964.

Sternloff, Robert Elmer, *The Critical Requirements for School Administrators Based Upon an Analysis of Critical Incidents.* Unpublished Ph.D. dissertation, University of Wisconsin, 1953.

Vines, Eugene T., *Community Service Programs in Selected Public Junior Colleges.* Unpublished Ed.D. dissertation, George Peabody College for Teachers, 1960.

Index